Mad Speculations

Reimagining Canada

Series Editors
Gregory Betts, Carl Everton James and Ian McKay

VOLUME 1

Concetta Principe

Mad Speculations

Anne Carson's Messiahs and the Canadian Unconscious

PETER LANG
New York · Berlin · Bruxelles · Chennai · Lausanne · Oxford

Bibliographic information published by the Deutsche Nationalbibliothek
The German National Library lists this publication in the German National Bibliography; detailed bibliographic data is available on the Internet at http://dnb.d-nb.de.

Library of congress control Number: 2025026413

Cover Image: 'Prose of the Trans-Canada'

ISSN 3042-7738
ISBN 978-1-63667-904-4 (print)
ISBN 978-1-63667-905-1 (ePDF)
ISBN 978-1-63667-906-8 (ePUB)
DOI 10.3726/b21722

Published by Peter Lang Ltd, New York (United States)

info@peterlang.com

This publication has been peer reviewed.

www.peterlang.com

Contact for General Product Safety Regulation (GPSR): gpsr@peterlang.com

Contents

Introduction

Anne Carson's experiments with genre, the unique hybrid forms of her work, tend to be the primary focus of scholarship, making an interest in what she is saying secondary. Noted is that the religious content of her work has had very modest attention. Perhaps secular embarrassment is the cause of this modesty. The fact is, Carson is a poet who happens to be compelled to consider aspects of religion that are troubling. For example, who hasn't wondered if a prophet in ancient biblical times who heard the word of God would be considered a psychotic by today's standards? This is the very conundrum she reflects on in her long poem "The Book of Isaiah." In *Autobiography of Red*, we might ask why wouldn't a red Greek winged beast, the protagonist who has been resurrected for her novel, be queer and on the spectrum? In the sequel, *Red Doc>*, a host of would-be saviors, gathered in a psychiatric institution located in some "nowhere," several existing in some uncanny "eternity," vie for our attention. In other words, her genre-bending tendencies are iterated by what she is doing with the content: in her work the postmodern schizophrenic, as defined by Frederic Jameson, is fused to a messianic expectation which, in Linda Hutcheon's terms, may be said to be deconstructing the modernist idea of salvation. Carson's work is littered with the figure that I define as the mad messiah. Further to the postmodern interest in deconstructing grand narratives that we live by unconsciously, this project will consider to what extent Carson's mad messiahs are deconstructing the grand narratives of salvation underpinning the Canadian unconscious.

One of the predominant strategies in Carson's work is irony, a strategy that raises questions for Canadian poet, Mary di Michele. In her interview with Anne Carson in 1996 for *Matrix Magazine*, di Michele takes issue with her irony being "unstable": What does she mean by unstable, anyway? In what situations would you find a "stable" irony? It is only by putting pressure on what di Michele might mean by irony, that we notice that di Michele is reflecting an aesthetic prejudice for the unambiguous as opposed to the ambiguous of postmodern projects. Where di Michele prefers a modernist stable irony, Carson plays with meaning so that two truths resonate or, in fact, keep spinning. This is the kind of trouble that reviewer Adam Kirsch attributes to the senselessness of words in Carson's work, a strategy inspired by de Saussure's contribution to linguistics, where the word is an arbitrary sign for the thing. So if Kirsch can complain that Carson's work is all about "sticking a monkey wrench in the gears of language" to accomplish some "heroic sabotage" (3 of 9), what are the gears and what is being sabotaged in Carson's "Glass Essay," for example, when she writes about a woman's effort to seduce her husband with "the little burning red backside like a baboon"?

Carson's "baboon" is the furthest you can get from heroic sabotage. The narrator's desire is equated to an animal, destabilizing and so critiquing the grand narrative of human superiority over the ape (evolution), by then destabilizing that critique with a critique of a woman's desire as "shame." Two registers are competing for dominance and neither wins, causing this movement we might call spinning. We see this similar ironic instability in Carson's reference to "hemorrhoids" in her homage to Samuel Becket, a detail which di Michele claimed was in "bad taste" (11). There is this push and pull of private and public registers, that arouses discomfort in the reader, but also, a little confusion about which side the text is on: is bad taste a good thing or a bad thing? Linda Hutcheon notes: "It is the function of irony in postmodern discourse to posit that critical distance and then undo it" (15). The critical distance of shame is destabilized by the baboon; the critical distance of "bad taste" is destabilized by "hemorrhoids." The discomfort aroused by the moving lines of the border of good and bad, so to speak, raises serious questions for di Michele, perhaps more seriously so because of her feminist politics. Equating a woman's desire with a baboon that is shameful really does pull the political floor out from under her. A woman's desire is either animalistic, and joyful, or it is suppressed and shameful. One of these positions would make sense for di Michele: together, there is only "unstable irony."

Irony is central to Carson's mad messiahs: if they are mad, they are not messiahs; if they are messiahs, they are not mad. To be both means that both conditions apply at the same time, making the irony unstable. The quandary raised by this figure has a precedent in historical figures. For example, Daniel Paul Schreber was a nineteenth-century German Judge who had revelations about the end of the world and thus recognized his messianic calling. He was the first diagnosed schizophrenic because he was deluded by his messianic mission. Another nineteenth-century figure, Louis Riel, considered himself a savior of the Métis people. Some say that his lawyers only claimed he was insane to save him from execution for treason, but others contend he was just simply mad. Would Riel be considered mad, like Schreber, because he saw himself as a messiah? Was Schreber a messiah despite being mad? One could speculate, and I will speculate in the pages ahead, that the historical precedent informs not only Carson's postmodern experiments with form, but also with character.

Her interest in mad figures nods to Jameson's embrace of the schizophrenic as the model of the postmodern subject. In his terms, the mad figure liberates us from the status quo; brings equality where there is inequality; brings freedom where there are chains. In Carson's hands, though, madness is the master narrative she critiques. The tendency is to think that mad people are irrational and not useful for society. Schreber was institutionalized because he was no longer fit to be a judge; Riel's execution affirms that his mission made him a threat to the Canadian government which is why he was deemed mad. In Carson's representation, not only is it compelling to consider psychosis as being receptive to God's revelation, but also worthwhile seeing living and breathing messiahs as figures who have challenged the dominant culture and thereby changed the course of history for the better. Schreber established a vision of schizophrenia because of his detailed *Memoirs of My Nervous Illness*; Riel's struggles eventually made possible the establishment of Métis status. If we accept Carson's logic of the relation between psychosis and revelation, we might also consider that psychosis is not a static state, but fluid: at times there are coherent revelations, at times not. And psychosis can instigate great changes to the status quo. That is, while Carson is carrying out a postmodern objective in a Jamesonian sense, you could say that Carson may be said to support Mad Studies in critiquing the neurotypical stigma against psychosis.

The messiah is a phenomenon that has been hailed by Hutchison as a modern project: it is easily a target for postmodernism. But why we even have a religious concept in our secular age is the question that is worth asking. The messiah is a first century phenomenon, defined by the Judean need for liberation from Roman oppression. In my monograph, *Secular Messiahs and the Return of Paul's Real* (2015), I have shown a connection between the contemporary use of the messiah and first century Judean thought. As I argue, there is a compulsive quality to this messiah's return in secularism that is symptomatic of trauma. In Lacan's terms, because trauma is a shock, it can never be witnessed when it is happening. That is, the event is "repressed," or stored in the unconscious. Because there is no memory of what happened, trauma is only apparent in the symptom of "return." But the return of the trauma is, you can say, in "disguise": for example, someone may come to realize that all the people they have fallen in love with have been narcissists: one narcissist is not the same as another narcissist, but over time, the several versions of narcissism indicate unconsciously driven behavior by the subject that follows a particular fantasy of what love is. The unconscious behavior is the fantasy that, you can say, processes a trauma. I argue in my monograph that the messiah is the fantasy that returns compulsively in secularism and signifies a trauma that we can date to the first century about social injustice. Taking this as my premise in the pages ahead, I suggest that the unconscious impulses informing Carson's representations of the mad messiahs, their differences acknowledged, may indicate a trauma of injustice central to contemporary Canadian society.

Seeing a connection between Carson's work and the Canadian unconscious is inspired by Sigmund Freud's analysis of culture. In *Moses and Monotheism*, Sigmund Freud attempts to explain contemporary anti-Semitism as a historical phenomenon which reflects the Jew's unconscious guilt for a historical murder: specifically, the murder of the first Moses, who was an Egyptian, who was replaced by a second Moses, the Midianite (49). Moses admits that this radical theory is based on weak textual "traces of a tradition" that historian Ernst Sellin observed in Prophet Hosea (42) pointing to a violence, or murder, against Moses: this murder, Freud claims, is a trauma which manifests as a historical guilt that returns in the second Moses, then in Jesus's death, and continues into the present as anti-Semitism, the irrational persecution of the Jews. Freud admits his analysis is "scarcely"[1] probable in explaining the unconscious reasons for the irrational persecution of the Jewish people for hundreds of years, yet he defends his work as useful because it initiates discussion and more research. The same impulse drives this work: speculation does not claim to be fact or truth: but it can indicate a probability that is worth considering and pursuing with more research.

In psychoanalysis, the question motivating analysis is what is the unconscious saying? The unconscious speaks in riddles or otherwise patterns such as slips of the tongue, ellipses, puns, contradictions, repetition, etc. The recurring figure of the messiah in Anne Carson's work is a pattern that inspires what I am doing in this project. In the pages ahead, I speculate on what the recurring figure could be saying about her unconscious. Moreover, just as Freud interpreted textual material to express a social unconscious, so I shall explore what Carson's messiah might tell us about the Canadian unconscious. In short, what you are about to read is perhaps "scarcely" probable, speculative as it is; nevertheless, I would argue it is worth considering because it may give us a way to reimagine the landscape of thought on Canada's culture.

To grasp the details of the trauma represented by Carson's mad messiah, we need to consider what master narratives drive Canadian identity, what ideologies need deconstructing using postmodern strategies. For that matter, what might we find indicative of a nationalism in Carson's work, the social and political realities within the imaginary boundaries as defined by Benedict Anderson. According to Marshal McLuhan, "Canada is the only country in the world that knows how to live without an identity." It is compelling to consider to what extent this lack of identity determines Carson's mad messiahs: do her messiahs exemplify a particular Canadian-ness? On the other hand, do

1 "We have scarcely achieved more than probability" Moses and Monotheism (164).

her messiahs reflect political realities such as the "two solitudes," the Franco and Anglo communities that are foundational to this nation, or as Jose Igartua describes in *The Other Quiet Revolution*, two quiet revolutions, one being the Québécois and the other its mirror in Anglo Canada? When it comes to race, how much of what is Canadian in the mad messiahs reflects the dominant white settler culture and in what case would the figure represent an ethnic minority of multiculturalism, as defined by Daniel Coleman in *White Civility*? Igartua and Coleman offer distinct trajectories that give some perspective on what we might look for in exploring the ideologies of race and nationalism in Carson's mad messiahs.

But there is one other grand narrative sustaining Canada that we need to keep in mind. While Anglo Canada is under threat politically and culturally by the United States and Britain, giving the nation what some have defined as an inferiority complex, this demographic sustains itself by believing that it has good relations with indigenous people evident in its treaties and its policies. In the history books taught in schools, this narrative has been sustained until recent changes to the curriculum have provided a slightly less biased story. Much of the First Nations history and issues with Canada had been buried until the Truth and Reconciliation Commission made them public; even then, there is little effort to uncover and stop the abuse against and murder of indigenous women; there is still no interest in addressing unceded territories. But above all, we must acknowledge that we are all complicit in reinforcing the narrative on which this nation is built, one that hides the theft of this land from, and the violent crimes against, indigenous people, by simply living here, owning property, naming ourselves Canadian. These historical and ideological perspectives on Canada's national narratives are fair targets for Carson's mad messiahs. Or to put it as a question: is Anne Carson, the poet, aware of these grand narratives in her work?

Postmodernism

In the poem, "The Anthropology of Water," Carson acknowledges that confronting her father's "word salad" (119), introduced her to a break in her world: "To live with a mad person requires many small acts of genius—reverse of the moment when Helen Keller shouts

'Water!'—when you glance at the mad world and suddenly see how it works" (122). The mad world of her father's last days in the family house are central to Carson's use of anthropology for her poetic message, not as a science, but as a procedure of "encounter": "encounter" with the other brings her face to face with the inexplicable: "Father had always been a private man. Now his mind was a sacred area where no one could enter or ask the way" (121). That "sacred area," the unknown world of her father's lost reality, erases her from his consciousness. Thus invisible, she can witness his life without interfering in it. So Carson, the poet, who sees her father living with dementia, may be seen to witness characters such as Geryon, Sad, 4NO, who one may consider are on the spectrum; also representative of madness are her works on Beckett,[2] Kafka, Holderin,[3] Artaud,[4] Weil,[5] and Bronte,[6] as well Deneueve,[7] who's role as a woman suffering a psychotic break in Polanski's *Repulsion* (1965) was, I suppose, Carson's inspiration. And there is "Isaiah," the biblical prophet: in hearing God, he must have been "mad" in the clinical sense. In this assembly of characters, it is apparent that "madness" is a common theme in her work. It is so common, in fact, that we might consider "madness" the unspoken thesis of Carson's oeuvre.

What is striking and exciting about Carson's apparent thematic unity is that it is tied closely to her genre-bending practice that is associated with postmodern strategies. Postmodernism is a term whose ambiguous definition centers on its dialogue with modernism: that prefix, "post," signals the "more" of modernism as much as it signals the "after." If modernism meant to reinvent tradition for the "now" of an industrialized society, postmodernism stepped in to problematize that tradition. That problematizing in post-World War Two cultural and theoretical practice is reflected in distrusting, and so disabling, those grand narratives that were so dear to the modernists. These are the basic ideas articulated by Jean-Francois Lyotard in his essay,

2 "Becket on Tragedy" and "Becket on Comedy."
3 "Short Talk on Kafka on Holderlin.
4 "TV Men: Artaud."
5 *Decreation.*
6 "Glass Essay."
7 "Irony is not Enough: Essay on My Life as Catherine Deneuve."

"The Postmodern Condition" a paper commissioned by *Conseil des universités du Québec* in 1979.

In 1982, Frederic Jameson's *Postmodernism: Or the Cultural Logic of Late Capitalism*, would be a more engaged and thorough reflection on the cultural movement. In his terms, postmodernism tackled modernism's selective memory as rooted in this trust in a tradition of the original, idyllic, authentic subject. A postmodernist would recognize that the present is not the fulfillment of the past, that there is no such thing as progress, and that there is no original natural order; everything is mediated by representation and we are caught in the simulacra of our thinking. That thinking reflects such a radical break with the past that the stable relationship between the past and the future falls apart on what Jameson suggests is a collective amnesia, reinforced by the engine of capital production. Working class history has long been lost. So, if the past is gone, and the future has no precedent, all that is left is the present of capital: an endless "present" that becomes the core of the "deep logic" of postmodernism's self-conscious engagement with process. Work is a product of the now; art is its own process; art is an artifact processed for consumption. In Jameson's terms, we see this exemplified in Andy Warhol's strategy of re-constituting capital, food brands or film stars, in products such as Campbell's soup or Marilyn Monroe. This very processing of the "now," may be considered so ubiquitous in postmodern culture, that there is no surprise in finding it in Carson's reflection on her father's condition as changing her relationship to being: she writes in "Anthropology of Water" that, in facing her father's condition, she "became interested in presence" (122). What is "presence" other than that state of "now" central to the processed quality of postmodernism?

Jameson's review of the postmodern project is especially important in this reading of Carson's work, for a few reasons. For one, Jameson's observations about postmodernism are indebted to Jacques Lacan's psychoanalysis. Where Lacan observes in clinical practice the symptoms that bring the analysand to the couch, Jameson puts onto that cultural couch postmodernism and identifies symptoms in that literary movement associated with strategies of self-referentiality. Thus, in postmodernism, "... any observation about the present can be mobilized in the very search for the present itself and pressed into service as a symptom and an index of the deeper logic of postmodernism" (xii). In Jameson's terms, the deeper logic is simply that history, so forgotten or repressed, returns in compulsive work such as Warhol's Campbell's soup or Marilyn Monroe's image. The past is so dissociated from the present, that all that remains is the time-related symptom of "now," a state typical of schizophrenia.

Jameson sees schizophrenia as emblematic of postmodernism, using the psychoanalytic definition of the disorder as a guide: "Lacan describes schizophrenia as a breakdown in the signifying chain, that is, the interlocking syntagmatic series of signifiers which constitutes an utterance or a meaning" (26). The postmodernist "breakdown" referenced signals how the schizophrenic mind is different from the Oedipalized subject's mind. When the Oedipalized subject speaks, they are not only communicating, they are also showing an organized relationship to language, a trust that words can mean. Oedipalized subjects know who they are, can speak for themselves, and have memories which means they have history. That is, not only do words have power to mean, but time is under control of a mind that remembers and plans for a future. In other words, the Oedipalized subject may be said to be the modern subject who has bought into the master narrative of progress, where there is a tomorrow building on a yesterday.

In contrast, the schizophrenic exists without that "master narrative," or specifically, the "master signifier" that purportedly allows them to make meaning. As such, the schizophrenic lives in "a rubble of distinct and un-related signifiers" which isolates the subject from social norms of communication and serves to destabilize markers of time. When the subject is thus "isolated, that *present* suddenly engulfs the subject with indescribable vividness, a materiality of perception properly overwhelming, which effectively dramatizes the power of the material—or better still, the literal—signifier in isolation" (emphasis mine 27). Jameson claims these "symptoms" of schizophrenia are everywhere in postmodern culture. The schizophrenic untangles the chain of signifiers from their etymological roots so that process is articulated in things that are unconnected or even "exploded." Schizophrenic art destroys the grand narratives of progress and thereby liberates us from the chains of the past.

Semantic and generic discontinuities, Jameson stresses, exemplify the paradox of postmodern culture not as a condition of nihilistic chaos, but as the ecstasy of psychosis:

> But I mainly wanted to show the way in which what I have been calling schizophrenic disjunction or *écriture*, when it becomes generalized as a cultural style, ceases to entertain a necessary relationship to the morbid content we associate with terms like schizophrenia and becomes available for more joyous intensities, for precisely that euphoria which we saw displacing the older affects of anxiety and alienation. (29)

The affects are effects of modernism, brought on by the narratives of progress in industrialization, urbanization, and globalization. The postmodern euphoria, the symptom of psychosis, are evocative of the one that, in breaking with the master narratives, is liberated.

Carson's focus on madness puts her work square in the field of Jameson's definition of postmodernism. Formalistically, her work also emulates what Linda Hutcheon interprets as the Canadian postmodern. The self-reflexive strategy of the style you can say is as simple as Atwood's "self-conscious" writing where the "the narrator in the Handmaid's Tale anguishes over the status of her narrative: "It isn't a story I'm telling" ... yet "It's also a story I'm telling" (17). In comparison to Atwood's work, Carson's generic oeuvre stands out as extremely self-conscious. The essay that is actually a poem, or the tango that is an essay, or the novel that is actually a poem, or the poem that is prose, are all examples of how the "form" or formula of culture in Carson's hands, unravels, bends, breaks, splits, and becomes reconstituted as a force that Jameson would say frees us from capital. In Hutcheon's terms, the troubling of form also frees us:

> Instead of feeling threatened by this unfixing of certainties, postmodern culture tends to find it liberating and stimulating. Perhaps the loss of the modernist faith in fixed system, order, and wholeness can make room for new models based on things once rejected: contingency, multiplicity, fragmentation, discontinuity. (19)

Notable is that what Hutcheon defines as postmodernism's formal strategies are emblematic of Jameson's idea of schizophrenic art. These ideas are embodied in *Autobiography of Red: A Novel in Verse*, a lyric work identified as a novel, involving a protagonist, Geryon, the ancient Greek semi-divine red beast with wings, who is obviously an anti-hero and on the spectrum and queer. Does Carson's work translate the American postmodern schizophrenic through Canadian generic innovations? That shall be considered in the chapter on *Red Doc>*, the sequel to "*Autobiography of Red*". For now, what is clear is that Carson's interest in the mad subject liberates us from something. The question is, what is that something?

The Mad Messiah

For a number of reasons that I shall explain now, I associate the schizophrenic with the revolutionary figure in twentieth century philosophy and political writing named the "messiah." The figure is central to the political activism of the materialist historian, Walter Benjamin, in his "On the Concept of History." But Benjamin's messiah is a modernist project: success or progress is inevitable, even if it must rely on that supra-human "moment in time" as "the gate through which the messiah will pass." Moving into the postmodern period, Jacques Derrida's engagement with the messiah is a self-conscious, deconstructive, reading of the Marxists narrative. Derrida's messianic is not even a figure, but the possibility of liberation that is always deferred. Etienne Balibar and Giorgio Agamben, two political philosophers, also take up the messianic promise in their writing. The figure fights for social justice without the baggage associated with Jesus and Christianity, making it a compelling term for secular discourse.

Designed in the eighteenth century, secularism was meant to separate church from state, thereby freeing the state from conforming to outdated and unnecessarily restrictive church demands. Moreover, this liberation meant that the state could support the needs of all subjects, irrespective of faith. In turn, the citizens could practice their faith in the privacy of their home without the anxiety of being persecuted. In secularism, religion has not been erased: it has simply been repressed from the public sphere. This would suggest that the messianic figure in contemporary political philosophy is a return of the repressed religious ideas of salvation. In my monograph, I outlined in detail how the unconscious return of the messiah signifies the first century Judean's anxiety with end of times and oppression by Roman rule; the return of this figure signals a lack in the social contemporary. In keeping with postmodernism's critique of the master narrative, the cultural schizophrenic liberates us from oppressive structures that are unjust. Thus, the messianic figure is returning in secularism because of a lack of social justice represented by the dominant religious faith in the west: Christianity. In short, Carson's postmodern avatar is a mad messiah, aimed to free us from master narratives that perpetuate inequality and injustice. What will be of interest in the analyses ahead will be in considering where equality and justice are lacking in our Canadian climate.

Criticism with Jameson's appropriation of the mental health condition of schizophrenia for its metaphorical use in postmodernism has been vocal. This use has no bearing on the condition, critics say, a condition which affects people in very different ways, depending on the comorbid disorders for a given individual. Moreover, those who live with the condition experience it acutely. The literary work is no comparison. If someone with the disorder represents their own condition, they have a personal reason to do so. While the disrespect implied in the postmodernist use is to be recognized, something about the critique of postmodernism's authority, or lack of authority, could be problematized. For one, how do you decide who has authority? As a reader, it is difficult to pass judgment about an author's license to write from a particular position since a reader has limited access to the author's biography. Added to that, Carson is noted for resisting autobiographical readings of her work. These issues make it difficult for us to know if, in fact, Carson is a neurotypical postmodern writer exploiting a disorder or actually representing her neurodivergence in writing about the psychotic. As some of the analyses ahead will show, her mad messiahs will give us some guidance in determining Carson's authority to tell the story, or at least to help us speculate on authority. Thus, these issues of the exception and authority shall be kept in mind in carrying out an analysis of her work in the pages ahead.

Just as the mad messiahs are somewhat caught in the criticism of Mad Studies, so the characters are caught by other aspects of the author's identity such as race and nationality. What we know about Carson is that she is a white settler Canadian woman, born in Ontario, who worked in Montreal as a professor for 15 years, and then moved to the United States where she has remained, teaching and living. In other words, she carries a kind of dual status we need to be sensitive to: where we might hear a Canadian-ness, we might also hear an American-ness. Bearing in mind how little we know about her, the analysis of how her identity has bearing on the representation of psychosis is limited. But at this point we can ask: are her mad messiahs "white settler" because she is "white settler"? Is there something Canadian about these mad messiahs? Linda Hutcheon makes a case for seeing Canadian postmodernism in strategies such as parody, "that which both asserts and undercuts that which it contests" and irony, that which "refuses resolution of contraries" (4–7). Both strategies are prevalent in Carson's work, especially the "unstable ironies" that di Michele has identified. With respect to Carson's generic experiments, we can hear Hutcheon's reflection on the Canadian Postmodern tendency of "unfixing of certainties." Moreover, Ian Rae in *From Cohen to Carson: The Poet's Novel in Canada*, argues that the Canadian poet's novel is a hybrid lyric project, combining the novel with the long poem, a distinctly Canadian form as promoted by Dorothy Livesay in "Documentary: A Canadian Genre?" and Sharon Thesen, editor of the *Long Poem Anthology, old and new.* Besides considering these formalistic concerns, I am interested in looking at what grand narratives Carson's messianic figures, on the one hand, undermine and on the other, perpetuate. In that respect, is there something Canadian about Carson's mad messiahs, and thereby, do we see into the Canadian unconscious?

Reflecting on what her work can tell us about Canadian-ness is part of the objective of this project, which is why I would like to consider the postmodern critics who each resist associating a regionalism of the text to postmodern strategies. Christian Bök argues that the Avant Garde is a field of literature in Canada that is postmodern because of its very experimental quality, which Hutcheon does not take into account in her putatively postmodern examples of very traditional fiction (Atwood's work being an example). He also takes issue with Hutcheon's claim that "sense of 'place' generates style of 'voice', that the landscape of the country generates the zeitgeist of our culture" (95). This he claims is a fallacy of "bad sociology" (95). Frank Davey argues that Canadian postmodernism withdraws from specificities of identity: "There is no necessary connection between identity politics, racial community writing, gay and lesbian writing, and the epistemological radicality of literary postmodernisms" (16). I agree with Bök that there is an issue with "bad sociology," and I see Davey's point that Canadian postmodern texts are less interested in identity politics than they are in strategies of knowledge. In fact, Carson's works are populated by generic characters in nowhere places, supporting Davey's assessment. In my approach, I will try to avoid "bad sociology" in considering Carson's work; but I am also going to think critically about why Carson's worlds seem so very stripped of political features. What do we make of the generic quality of her characters, this anywhere of her locations? As I will argue in the pages ahead, the features of religion, region and even racial identity in Carson's mad messiahs, are more apparent in what is absent than what is present.

In the Pages Ahead

The limitations of my analysis are several. For one, I do not use all of Carson's work to carry out this study. Rather, I follow a connection between a theme of religious impulse in her work, and the psychotic subject in the projects spanning her oeuvre: specifically, her long poem "The Book of Isaiah" (1995), her novella *The Autobiography of Red* (1998), and then the sequel to this novella, *Red Doc>* (2013). In other words, there are significant reflections on the religious in *Plainwater, Glass, Irony and God*, and in *Desecreation*, that I do not explore. What I am interested in considering is the shift from her focus on religious texts (Isaiah) to her treatment of ancient Greek fragments about a demi-god (Geryon), to her parody of Greek drama (R*ed Doc>*). In the biblical material, the prophet has basically been diagnosed as a schizophrenic; in the pronounced anti-Oedipal exception, Geryon is introduced as an autistic queer subject who matures (socializes) into the beautiful winged beast of his post-Herakles break up; in *Red Doc>*'s psych ward, we see a pantheon of characters each suffering a condition, whether it is PTSD, anxiety disorder or manic depression, among others. The narrative I see in this selection reflects a kind of reinvention of what I am defining as the Noth American postmodern "schizophrenic" along the lines of the psychotic spectrum which I would say describes an arc of the postmodern movement in Canadian culture.

Before analyzing the three texts, I start this project looking at Carson's relationship to religion as articulated through the interview conducted by a decidedly non-postmodern writer, Mary di Michele. The dynamic between them in the interview, in fact, makes for some very dramatic reading, in which there are moments when we hear Carson's silence so clearly it has an impact on di Michele who comes to realize her failure to conduct a good interview. The drama is more obvious for me, and outlined in my interpretation here, because of my conflicted relationship to di Michele and my artistic devotion to Carson. *Short Talks* was the first book I read by Carson, and I fell in love with it as it was doing exactly what I was aiming for in my own prose poems. While doing my M.A. in creative writing at Concordia, I had Mary di Michele as a supervisor for my creative dissertation and not surprisingly, she had "many problems" with my work. I had personal experience of di Michele's dislike of postmodernist writing which is articulated in spades in this interview she conducts with Carson, and I use my knowledge in my analysis of the dialogue. But the critical element of this dialogue is how di Michele avoids Carson's reflection on religious thinking: it is this reflection that I take up in my analysis because, as mentioned earlier, so little has been written about it.

The chapter also contextualizes how we might read Carson's work as feminist, in terms of Linda Hutcheon's analysis of the postmodern feminist, followed by an exploration of ideology in Carson's work. What does secularism have to do with her mad messiahs? Do her mad messiahs show a Canadian-ness, as in a national ideology, and do they support or undermine it? And further, do we see an undermining of the racial identity in the figures represented, or an avoidance of the racial master narrative? This focus on certain ideologies sets the stage for the analysis ahead in which I distinguish features of the white Anglo-Saxon (WASP) settler privilege in Carson's mad messiahs, grounded in both Canada's founding history and the rise of political discourse in secularism.

In the long poem, "Book of Isaiah," I will be concentrating on how Carson shows an equation between the prophet and the psychotic: in tradition, encounters with God were revered as divine experiences, while today, those encounters would be considered the hallucinations of a schizophrenic. So, in writing the biblical narrative as a secular project,

Carson destabilizes the prophetic tradition while also raising questions about stigma against the schizophrenic. The representation begs the question: is there some trace of sectarianism in this representation? That question can be posed because I have argued in my monograph, *Secular Messiahs and the Return of Paul's Real*, that secular ideology is not just a system of a new belief order, as put in place by enlightenment ideals, but is, in fact, a system modeled on Christian principles. More recent scholarship (Joseph Blankholm) argues that secularism is modeled on Protestant concepts, such as skepticism of rituals and iconoclasm. This Christianization of the state disguised as secularism is rehabilitated by Carson's treatment of Isaiah. That is, the Jewish Isaiah has historically been Christianized; in Carson's secularization of the prophet through her postmodern schizophrenic, he is not just Christianized, but Protestant-ized. As I will show, the mad messiah reinforces a Christian master narrative with Protestant features signaling a conflation of both Canadian and American cultures. The other interesting ideological layer in this poem is Carson's enigmatic engagement with feminisms.

The chapter focused on *Autobiography of Red*, explores how Geryon, the red winged demi-god beast of Greek mythology, is reinvented as queer and autistic: as a child he is extremely shy (mute?) because he has wings, beast that he is; he suffers synesthesia, that allows him to see grass as red thus overwhelmed by the imaginary; he has trouble reading maps or navigating the symbolic order. Geryon's story is one of socialization (Oedipalization) through love, enabled by the technology of photography: through photographs, Geryon tells his "autobiography." This self-generated narrative carried out through the spectral order of photos is the means by which Geryon moves out of the autistic spectrum to Oedipalization. Using photography, Geryon saves himself from social isolation, and in that way, becomes the savior (messiah) of himself, and then his friends. The implications of this in terms of Mad Studies are many. For one, why does Geryon need saving? For another, where Geryon putatively saves himself with photographs, the conceit is only possible because of the narrator: a witness figure who, in returning Geryon's gaze through the metaphor of the photograph, gives Geryon the site/sight for being resurrected from his bestial origins. In other words, Geryon passes through the mirror stage to Oedipalization thanks to a narrator who we may see as reinforcing a neurotypical desire for the cure against the lived experience of autism.

The chapter on *Red Doc>* explores what initially seems like the failure of this sequel of *Autobiography of Red*, and in failing to be one, indicates a postmodern strategy. Whether or not that was Carson's intention, it works, in that sense. Another postmodern strategy can be seen in the multiple disorders of characters whose storylines take up space and interfere in the narrative. The tempo is so frenetic and the cacophony so profound that it is tempting to suppose the multiple personalities are just the voice of the narrator who, as an organizing principle, is the protagonist: a kind of interpretation of Pirandello's six characters in search of an author, in which the narrative moves forward without focus until the story is found. In *Red Doc>*, that discovery is made at the end of the novel as Geryon's mother lays dying. I propose the narrator, with its multiple personalities, embodies features of a mad messiah who fails to save their mom from her mortal end.

In the conclusion, I reflect on which grand narratives are problematized by the mad messiahs, and which remain unbroken. That unbrokenness, I say, despite all the radical postmodern artistic feats, indicates a conservative quality to her work, one that is determined by the long shadow of Anglo settler sensibility expressed in the motto "Good Governance" which riddles the Canadian unconscious, and which probably still animates some of the Anglo language literature in Canada. I am also interested to see to what extent the Canadian culture of this text is determined by a US sensibility, if we can even see that distinction in the analysis ahead.

Modernism Vs. Postmodernism

I had been reading Anne Carson's work for decades by the time I had read David Solway's "The Trouble with Annie." It is an article in which Solway condemns Carson's work as bad while infantilizing her by referring to her as "Annie." I was surprised by the lack of restraint in his diatribe against "Annie," unselfconsciously revealing his apparent *jouissance* with his hate-on for Carson's work. Solway notes the "lack of fiber" of her lyric and criticizes "Freud (First draft)" as mere "disjointed locutionary tagmemes" (24). Overall, the "deficiencies … inevitably subtend in the pseudo-cerebrality of the intellectual mountbank (26)." There is too much "mental" work in her writing, and it is this very mental work that he condemns. Notice the relish with which Solway describes his distaste for her work. Notice that his zest for adjective speaks more about his aesthetic prejudices than it does about her contribution to Canadian poetry.

Adam Kirsch's review of Carson's *Autobiography of Red* is condemning in ways similar to Solway's critique:

> Carson neither feels her thoughts, nor thinks her feelings. Yet it is the role of poetry to bring these two halves of experience together, a fusion which is made possible by translating moments of being into musical patterns of words. Lacking a commitment to the rigor of such patterns—a commitment to verse—Carson attains neither poetry's music nor poetry's wisdom. (9 of 9)

Notice how Kirsch uses a paradox to introduce a very traditional idea of what poetry is supposed to do. What poetry does, according to Kirsch, is "fuse" and make whole the elements of the paradox and carries that out with musical patterns fulfilling everything with the apotheosis: wisdom. This is a very modernist definition of poetry and clearly in conflict with Carson's postmodern wordplay, one he associates with Stein and "emptying out language" (2 of 9), in "defense of nonsense" (3 of 9). Kirsch believes that good poetry is good because it relies on meaning. Moreover, according to Kirsch, Carson's "postmodern free verse" is "too much like tennis with the net down" (4 of 9). In effect, her poetry may look like poetry, but it is not working as poetry. In this accumulation of critical observations, we understand that Kirsch's idea of poetry honors tradition and means something, as indicated by his comparison of Carson to the early modernist, Gerald Manley Hopkins. The difference between Solway's diatribe and Kirsch's review is that the former has a personal investment in condemning Carson's work, while the latter offers a more reliable critical response. In one sense, though, Solway and Kirsch are the same: they judge Carson's work in comparison to traditional poetry of which they have some expertise. They "know" poetry, and Carson's work does not fit the definition.

The critique exhibited by these two scholars was common among many poets, and more so with the Canadian readership than American: Carson was ignored by Canada's literary scene until her reputation in the United States grew enough to warrant accolades and awards, thus leading to an ambivalent acceptance of her work in Canada. Things have changed in the past few decades, since she has garnered the distinction of being the first writer to win two Griffin awards. The seat of this earlier ambivalence is unclear, but the reason for it may be deduced from things said in an interview Mary di Michele did with Carson for *Matrix Magazine* (49), in 1996. In that interview, di Michele is less a critic than a poet in her reading of Carson's work. That "reading" inspired a dialogue between them that I would venture to say embodies the very conflict outlined by Solway's Annie article, with equal *jouissance*, you might say, and with far more drama.

Unstable Irony

The exchange between di Michele and Carson began entirely normally, touching on issues of prose and poetry, genre and "convention," and even the requisite reference to feminist politics—requisite because second wave feminism was in full force in academia at the time and di Michele was a new professor at Concordia and was surrounded by an astounding community of writers expounding "feminisms," including Nicole Brossard, Gail Scott and Erín Moure. There was a general tension in the exchange between di Michele and Carson, but that tension became more pronounced when di Michele started to raise questions about "Anthropology of Water." This is a long poem, in *Plainwater*, divided into several movements of first person confessions, ranging from a piece about her father's slow descent into dementia until his death, to two pilgrimages, one to Campostela with El Cid and another across the United States to Los Angeles with "the Emperor of china," finishing with "Swimming with my Brother," a poem about her brother who had at that point estranged himself from the family. Perhaps Carson was just not prepared to get into the emotional undertow in "Anthropology," since what exactly happened in the exchange between di Michele and Carson is unclear, except that something happened which remains a bizarre moment and happened like this: di Michele opened up a cavern and Carson fell in. Or did Carson pretend to fall in? Did Carson outline the "cavern" that a green interviewer did not recognize and trap the interviewer in seeing the "effect" by "pretending to fall in"? And di Michele, missing the hole, did fall in? Even now, after re-reading this interview, I am not sure what exactly happened... Something was opened and in that echoing new space of the discussion, there was a falling.

It started with di Michele identifying a contradiction in Carson's Beckettian reference in "The Anthropology of Water" in which "details are in bad taste" (223). Following this reference, di Michele notes that the narration is filled with detail including, "Fumigating my haemorrhoids"... which might make one cry out, to quote the much quoted line from the film *Pulp Fiction*: 'That was more than I needed to know'" (11), di Michele adds, finishing with: "What do we need to know [about your art of storytelling]?" (11) Carson's response to the query seems an over-reaction: "Most of my writing has been a mistake and (as you point out) tasteless. Writing draws one into indecency. I don't know why. I would retract everything if I could." The last statement is such an uncommonly weak moment for Carson that I suspect she is playing, and even then,

I cannot be sure that she has not actually been hurt by di Michele. Was she baiting di Michele or caving into an apparent criticism? What was the tenor of her voice? Was she being ironic or sincere? That is never answered since di Michele launches into an immediate retraction, indicating she had taken Carson seriously; but rather than retreat with a light joke or even just finish with the apology, "I did not mean in any way to suggest your writing is tasteless," di Michele advances (some might hear attacks) with her questions, by introducing a quotation from yet another project, "The Glass Essay": "It seems to me that your work moves, engages, through its dissonances: the rarified intellect, meditations on ideas and literary texts, along with naked flashes of the body, 'the little burning red backside like a baboon'. What struck me about the passages I'm referring to in the previously mentioned question is how unstable the irony is." Carson's response is documented as "—." I was totally impressed by the fact the silence was not edited out. And it was shocking, the silence. It roared.

We might suppose that di Michele misjudged Carson's emotional reaction to "bad taste" as sincere, since she pushes forward on her mission to understand what we need to know about Carson's writing so we can understand it and make Carson feel better about herself. There is a patronizing quality to this effort to make the interviewee feel better that one imagines riles Carson. Carson's silence in response to di Michele's wish for a confirmation that "unstable irony" is not a good thing, may have indicated any number of things, including the question I have raised about how manipulative di Michele is in introducing her trouble with unstable irony, especially insensitive since di Michele had called attention to Carson's idea of "bad taste" just minutes before. The possibility that Carson is parodying the "ideal interviewee," is one I think we should keep in mind, even if we cannot confirm what was actually happening for her at that moment in the interview. That di Michele makes an assumption about the interviewee is evident in her follow-up question to Carson's "silence": "What has been the critical response to your work?" Of course, di Michele may have been trying to give Carson the chance to dig herself out of the hole ("I would retract everything if I could"), if she had actually fallen into a hole. There was a lot of positive critical responses to her work to reference, since she was an established writer in the United States, with support by Guy Davenport at New Directions and even literary critic, Harold Bloom, and she was now a subject of an interview for the Canadian literary community. Yet the interview was, essentially over, since Carson answers with a series of one-liners in response to di Michele's repeated efforts to get Carson back, and seems to end abruptly after di Michele's condescending question (What question might you ask yourself?), with Carson's response: "But this is your interview, is it not?" (12). I wish I had been a fly on the wall to hear the silence resonating, the crossing of legs causing the flustering of bodies in fabric, fingers dragged through the hair and eyes bright with questioning. Was something edited here? Was there a limping to an end? Who "agreed" that this moment was the end of the interview?

Ironically, at the time that this interview was happening, Carson was writing *Autobiography of Red*, the project that would garner the very kudos that Kirsch would object to and that Solway would claim was not deserving of praise. di Michele's bizarre reflection on Carson's unstable irony is a part of that criticism. In short, this interview outlines an aesthetic confrontation between the lyrical modernist poets and the atonal postmodern writer, a confrontation that Carson faced and that I knew personally, having received feedback from di Michele about my own postmodern work. I do not consider myself an equal of Carson, especially since I could never manage to not fall into the pit of audience disgust with my work, but for a brief moment, I saw the value of having an avatar who can figure out how to solve all my lack of confidence problems. In general, however, it is the postmodern project that explains the kind of subject Carson is working with, and as I will outline soon, that subject brings us face to face with a Canadian unconscious and her mad messiahs.

The Politics of Feminism, the Politics of Postmodernism

When, in the interview with Carson, di Michele cites Irigaray's understanding of Logos as male-centered, in contrast to women's language which is "not rational, structured language" (9), di Michele appears to lead the conversation to a politics that she assumes is shared: the politics of feminism. She asks Carson what she thinks of Irigaray's feminist idea of "feminine language" versus the masculine "logos" (9). Carson shows, by defining in very clear terms Irigaray's position on what language is for women, that she knows more about Irigaray than her writing would lead us to assume, but admits that Irigaray's theory is not useful for her: "I find this writing hard to read and suspect I can learn very little from it" (10). A tension is growing between them that exposes the trench dividing the two literary movements. It becomes visible when Carson diverts the conversation about feminism and gender in another direction by reflecting on "the activity of praise and the function of worship. These are essential to human works of language" ... "Into the darkness of someone else's garden ..." (10). di Michele knows this quotation is from Pushkin and the religious ideas reflected there, but does not follow Carson's lead. Rather, she brings everything back to the issues she is interested in exploring. di Michele notices that the male figures in Carson's work are not real people but "mythopeic constructions" and wants to know why Carson does not use actual names but titles, such as "my Cid." The implication here is that Carson's work seems to be so abstract, unreal. Carson defends her use of nicknames such as "Tom, Dick or Harry" and then claims that "words after all are dead" (10). di Michele does not ask what Carson means but rather begins to answer her own question:

> Whether language is living or dead is for me problematic. In the mouth it is alive, on the page it is technological, perhaps. The mouth is silenced by death, but words, like hair, continue to grow for a while with the author. Don't you, yourself, mx the living and the dead when you choose to interview Mimnermos? (11)

"Mimnermos: The Brainsex Paintings" is a piece in *Plainwater*, that carries out a poem through a dialogue between interviewer and the ancient Greek poet. Di Michele uses an interesting ironic twist on the actual interview, by highlighting that voice of the dead in her use of "the living and the dead." Carson crushes the irony by flattening the space between word and meaning: "The mixture remains a verbal artefact, not animate." With simple logic, Carson shows that di Michele's observations are wrong and the aesthetic distance between them is massive. Shortly after this, di Michele would complain about "unstable irony."

As interesting as di Michele's critique of aspects of Carson's work is, di Michele's resistance to take up Carson's religious line of thought is more so. Early on in the interview, Carson reflects on the reasons that she is interested in Paul Celan, Emily Dickinson, Fernando Pessoa, and Gertrude Stein: "Economy and devotion interest me in these poets" (9). For a scholar intent on close-reading, I am intrigued by Carson's use of "devotion." She goes on to say, "And I believe that a fundamental motive of thinking and making stuff ... is worship. That is, apprehension of some larger than-oneself thing. And that is missing from a great deal of modern thought" (9). Ironically, di Michele ignores these interesting supposedly religious ideas, all begging for discussion, by getting technical: "What tools do you use for writing?" It is an odd question today, but at the time, it was a large part of the discussion of creative practice, as the computer was only just becoming a tool, and was much hated by people who preferred to write with pens or pencils. Carson uses the pen and pencil, for anyone interested. The fact that di Michele is more interested in tools for writing than in content of the writing stands out.

Why does di Michele not ask Carson what she means by "worship" or the "larger-than-oneself thing"? Why does di Michele not ask about Pushkin's poem or question what Carson means by "the activity of praise and the function of worship" (10)? These questions could have drawn out some discussion on the plethora of religious references in "Anthropology of Water," such as the pilgrimage to Campostela and the use of the rosary while on the American road trip to Los Angeles. We might suppose di Michele's silence on these religious allusions reflects the secular embarrassment with religious discussion in the public sphere. On the other hand, the silence might reflect an acceptance of faith as ubiquitous to the extent that nothing needs to be said and, in secular terms, that is your private affair. Either or both of these could explain di Michele's silence, though the possibility that di Michele was actually aiming to pose the question about "unstable irony," her agenda on the formalistic concerns reflected in modernism vs postmodernism, seems like a more likely reason for not asking about religion.

The extent to which di Michele avoided discussing Carson's "devotion," "praise," and "worship" because these terms were of less interest to her than feminisms, is the extent to which the following question has legs: does di Michele avoid the religious because it is too private to interrogate or too parochial to engage with critically? Are notions of privacy and parochialism prejudices underlying how we have been trained to live with religion in our secular world? As a poet and teacher at the university, working in an ostensibly secular community of feminist writers, di Michele probably felt there were two current and relevant topics of discussion: form, which was the debate between tradition and experimentation countering that tradition, today defined as modernism vs postmodernism, and the politics of feminisms, rooted in women's emancipation from patriarchy and misogyny. Ignoring prayer was a no brainer, since prayer was not going to give a woman the chance to be an equal in competition with men, nor undo the trauma of rape. With only eligible politics in her view, di Michele dove into the query around form, the relationship between politics and form.

What di Michele's critique of Carson's work showed is her own prejudices for a modernist aesthetic over postmodernism. The effect of her inquiry also exposed her prejudices about religion and faith which we need not interpret as di Michele confession of atheism, as much as it could be considered indicative of secular resistance. Religious concepts are private and do not belong at the secular university. Already, it is apparent how secularism is a grand narrative waiting for a postmodernist to come along and destabilize it. In the context of Carson's career, and especially her publications in the mid-1990s, *Plain Water* and *Glass, Irony and God*, the very private ideas of "prayer" and faith were being made public by Carson in some very dramatic ways. So while di Michele is focusing on trying to expose the weaknesses of the postmodern aesthetic from a modernist perspective, and, in search of a common feminist agenda to test the political waters of this literature that she is not convinced by, di Michele puts Carson into a corner and Carson responds with postmodern aplomb, parodying the interview by playfully recreating the drama of the Mimnermos interview found in *Plainwater.*

Postmodern Politics

The divide that opened up between di Michele and Carson in the interview, on the one hand, shows how aesthetic alliances inform all individual's conscious and unconscious responses to the reading of any given text, and on the other hand, highlights how ideology binds us to a certain position which can deafen us to what people are actually saying. We could say that di Michele meant to show inclusivity by engaging

Carson in issues central to feminist ideology, making the assumption that it was shared because Carson was a woman, after all. Carson was pushing back on this assumption and giving di Michele many opportunities to discuss other aspects of her writing and specifically, her religious ideas. So, what has been shown as the doubling of the tension between these two writers actually reflects a conflict between two fields: the aesthetic issues around modernist versus postmodernist strategies; the unspoken conflict between a feminist politics versus religion in a secular context.

Postmodernism's tendency to be associated with work that does not have a political agenda was addressed, to a certain extent, by Jameson's theory of the postmodernist project being a product of late capitalism. The fact that it defined an art that was cut-off from the memory of a class-based struggle meant for Jameson that it had betrayed its political origins. The supposed incommensurability between postmodernism's de-formalism and any political agenda is problematized by Linda Hutcheon in *The Politics of Postmodernism*. According to Hutcheon, postmodernism should be understood as a strategy: its formal concerns are not working against the artist's politics, nor are they inherently political. The artist, whether left or right politically, can still be considered postmodernist in approach. The strategy of demolishing the grand narrative remains viable for political critique, including by women artists who stand under a feminist banner. Hutcheon notes that, while postmodern aesthetics and feminist politics are projects that are essentially incommensurable, one maintaining an ambivalence and the other aiming for a particular change, the fact that they cannot be conflated does not mean that they cannot co-exist:

> 'Feminism is a politics'. Postmodernism is not; it is certainly not political, but it is politically ambivalent, doubly encoded as both complicity and critique, so that it can be (and has been) recuperated by both the left and the right, each ignoring half of that double coding. (163)

The reason that feminism and postmodernism cannot be conflated is because one is a politics and the other is a strategy. For that reason, a feminist can use the postmodern strategy of deconstructing a master narrative of patriarchy, for example, but introducing a new objective or a new master narrative would not be on the agenda.

Hutcheon problematizes the presumed incommensurability between postmodernism's de-formalism and modernist politics, while also acknowledging that postmodernism's targeted grand narrative is messianism itself:

> Postmodernism has called into question the messianic faith of modernism, the faith that technical innovation and purity of form can assure social order, even if that faith disregards the social and aesthetic values of those who must inhabit those modernist buildings ... Postmodern architecture is plural and historical, not pluralist and historicist; it neither ignores nor condemns the long heritage of its built culture—including the modern. It uses the re-appropriated forms of the past to speak to a society from within the values and history of the society, while questioning it. It is in this way that its historical representations, however parodic, get politicized. (11)

Whether we are speaking of modernist architecture, or modernist poetry, no work can be seen as outside the political; yet more interesting is how Hutcheon frames her observation around "messianic faith" which she defines as a distinctly modern idea. This is to say that, rather than focus on the trouble di Michele identifies in Carson's weak feminist politics, we might look into Carson's interest in the religious as a postmodern engagement with the modernist "messianic faith": that is, the mad messiah.

Notable in Hutcheon's reflection is how messianism has taken up real-estate in her secular scholarship. We can date it to the modernist works of Walter Benjamin. He was a historical materialist whose anti-Nazi-socialist politics lead to his writing "On the Concept of History." In that text, he believed that we could defeat Nazism with what he would define as "weak messianic power." Contemporary philosophers such as Giorgio Agamben and Jacques Derrida, all staunch secularists have had some investment in this figure, whether it is to deconstruct it, as Derrida does, or to problematize it as Agamben does. The use of "messianic" by any secular scholar/thinker/poet calls attention to a contradiction in secularism. How does a secular discourse accommodate this religious discourse except to question the promises secularism makes about religious freedom. The fact that there are many "messiahs" in Carson's work, though this may not initially seem obvious, confirms that there are master narratives to dismantle, one of which is secularism.

This dismantling of secular ideology through use of the messianic trope is the politics Carson engages in. Where Carson's messiahs are lurking and how she uses them to undermine Canadian grand narratives, can be explored only once I have had a chance to reflect on the ideologies fortifying her mad messiahs.

Secular Ideology

The only freedom a subject has, Slavoj Žižek claims, is to recognize the ideological system that has an impact on our choices, thinking and desires: that is, becoming conscious of the unconscious influences of ideology. As Žižek asserts in *The Sublime Object of Ideology*, ideology is an illusion: a fantasy of the coherent world we live in which we mistake for reality (45). What is positive and good about secularism is not secularism, but the fantasy that secularism delivers about itself, which, at the core, is centered on a contradiction (Žižek 50). Ideology works on the trick of the contradiction: the trick of secular ideology has many examples. Recently, a woman was told by the presiding government that her Niqab, a full-face cover, had to be taken off if she wanted to be sworn in as a Canadian citizen. The logic in this order is that Canadian citizens are equal. To come to the citizenship ceremony different from everyone else, emphasizes an inequality; this inequality is further exacerbated by the fact that she covers this way because of her gender. In short, for this woman to be a Canadian citizen, she must show herself as equal to other Canadians, even if it means that she loses the right to choose what she will wear when and she loses this doubly, because it is a white man who is telling her, the brown woman, what she needs. This is another case of what Gayatri Spivak targets as the colonialist misogynist authority that aims to have a white man "save the brown woman from the brown man" in her famous article "Can the Subaltern Speak?" As it turns out, the Canadian Supreme Court sided with the woman's wish to wear her Niqab and she became a citizen in time to help vote that prohibitive government out of office.

Secularism erases religious differences as the basis of equality. But as *Žižek* observes, every ideology has a contradiction built into it. In secularism, the promises are belied by the fact on the ground which is global inequality based on race, sex, age, and any other marker you can think of. Is this why Carson niggles away at religion in her secular work? In "The Truth About God" she mentions Rabbi Luria, a kabbalist; she explores the story of Isaiah the prophet in the poem of that title; in *Autobiography of Red*, she has gone pagan in centering her story on Geryon, a red Greek beast. This multiplicity of faiths, from monotheistic to pagan, would suggest she is targeting secular ideology as a master narrative for her postmodern objective. What interests me about Carson's work is her provocative engagement with secularism through the messiah.

Our modern association of the "mesiach," Hebrew for "chosen," with the figure who is the redeemer or savior, has very limited artifactual support in material history, but is most strongly attested to in the first century A.D., and specifically, the period of Jesus of Nazareth. While Jesus Christ, the messiah, historically brought into focus several socio-historical issues of the first century, specifically the persecution of the Judeans, religious, ethnic and class inequality, Christianity remains only a retrospective signifier of the salvationary expectations of contemporary Judeans. In other words, the story of Christianity assumes Judean principles to prove its "catholic" or universal function as God's faith and its rightful place as the successor to Judaism. That is, the Christian messiah was supposed to bring equality and freedom to those who were oppressed. In short, the "messianic" in secularism is the return of an ancient Christian promise. For this reason, I can support literary scholars Gill Anidjar's claim that "Christianity is secularism." What is striking in the analysis ahead is to see how a specific denomination (i.e., Protestantism) persists in the messianic representation which I will show indicates a Canadian identity.

Mad Studies

Ableism is an ideology that promotes itself as the norm. This has been made apparent by the Mad Studies movement, a relatively new field of study (mid-aughts) that has adapted methods of critique defined by disability studies. If disability studies could lobby against assumptions made by abled colleagues, Mad Studies highlights where able-minded thinking and projects unconsciously exclude the disabled. Scholars of the movement argue that equality fostered by feminist, Marxist, queer and racialized politics overlooks its inherent ableism. This ideology assumes that normal people are neurotypical which is to say that anyone with a disorder or other mental health condition is "abnormal" and in need of a cure or needs to be fixed. This ableist ideology that underlies most social justice politics has been questioned by a growing community of neurodivergent activists.

Scholars claim that cultural theorists and artists have in some circumstances exploited mental health conditions for cultural consumption. Moreover, Mad Studies critics have taken issue with the appropriation of the schizophrenic condition as a conceit for postmodernist liberation. In "The Unexceptional Schizophrenic: A Postmodern Introduction," Catherine Prendergast is critical of the way that postmodern theory reflects on the schizophrenic as an "exception:" by being singular and distinct, the trope entirely overlooks the reality of living as a schizophrenic. The experience is far from liberating, nor is the schizophrenic necessarily isolated by language difficulties. The fact is, the schizophrenic lives in community, an individual among others, whether that community is made up of family, fellow inmates, or an institution; and the schizophrenic lives in time. Regarding the postmodern project, Prendergast states: "What is common in these moments of access is the certitude with which schizophrenics are discussed; the schizophrenic is allowed no change in position or in thinking, and no agenda of her or his own" (234). In postmodern culture, then, the schizophrenic is a shorthand for something static and even inhuman. The reality is that every schizophrenic experiences their disorder differently, whether that is being stigmatized, living with co-morbidities, or taking medications, or all of these factors together, and making a life worth living. That is, there is no typical schizophrenic, nor can a list of symptoms reflect the unique nature of the individual's condition, those who have been and have not been diagnosed, who live with it and over time, through therapy and medication and age, develop a different relationship to their condition. Prendergast's argument is poignantly disturbing if we consider that the postmodern schizophrenic is considered a liberator when some schizophrenics are completely trapped by their condition. And then again, when we consider the experience of "trapped," are we working with ableist language, since many neurodivergent people feel trapped by having to follow an ablest agenda?

In postmodern art, the metaphorical value of the schizophrenic entirely overlooks the reality of people who are living with schizophrenia. Yet Prendergast's observation misses how the mad person might be valuable in political terms. The postmodern schizophrenic, or mad person, is the exception to the Oedipal rule, which in Agamben's terms is the Homo sacer, the one that can be killed with impunity but has a sacred/cursed value and brings out the ethical root of the conflict; the postmodern schizophrenic as the messianic is one of those powerful exceptions. It is powerful because it can bring new perspectives on old troubles; it is also powerful in being able to rewrite the pejorative language about madness. In other words, I am taking up this project on the postmodern messiah even with its inherent flaws in Mad Studies perspectives, because it is doing the work of postmodernism to abolish grand narratives. What grand narratives are coming apart in the messianic trope? And more importantly, what grand narratives remain intact?

In respect to Carson's work, I will highlight that each mad messiah I consider is a distinctive character that troubles the stereotypes replicated in the postmodern theorists' works: this is to say that where Jameson wants to define the postmodern strategy as schizophrenic, Carson's protagonists reflect on the master narratives that shore up the clinical definitions of those on the psychotic spectrum. As well, we see Geryon in two different time periods, showing that his relationship to his condition changes over time. Of course, we need to bear in mind here that the mad messiah remains a fantasy, a fictional construct; so even if the figure is modeled on someone living, Prendergast's reservations remain noteworthy, even if analyzing Carson's messiahs as articulating a political message is a worthy cause.

The other argument, as noted by Drew MacEwan in his dissertation, "Mad Futures Now: Avant-Garde Dishumanism in the Poetry of Claude Gauvrau, Hannah Weiner, and Bill Bissett," which is a much stronger criticism than Prendergast's, is that when the representation of the schizophrenic is being carried out by neurotypical subjects a disservice is occurring. This particular representation of madness mistakes the representation as giving voice to a heretofore silenced minority. What it is doing, in fact, is patronizing the minority. In assuming that putting the schizophrenic story into circulation is enough to change the culture of stigmas, the neurotypical writer makes assumptions about what is at stake for a neurodivergent subject, and thereby interferes in their opportunity to represent themselves. Moreover, the neurotypical author who assumes that they can articulate the condition better than one with a disability is arrogant, especially since there are many eloquent neurodivergent testimonies, creative and not. The argument being made boils down to the fact that, in Mad Studies scholarship, some have authority to tell the story, and some do not.

While these points are well observed, I have elsewhere raised questions with the authorial argument. For example, when we ask, "is Carson exploiting the schizophrenic subject for her art?" our query is assuming that Carson is neurotypical. But is she? In an article I wrote about Mark Haddon's apparent exploitation of the autistic subject for his novel *The Curious Incident of a Dog in the Nighttime,* I make the point that not only are we not in a position as readers to judge the author for their supposed neurotypical-ness, the author, themself, is sometimes not in a position to judge their own authority, if they simply do not know that they may have a condition or suspect they have a condition but have never been diagnosed. Recently, there have been more and more diagnoses of people in their middle age or older of being on the psychotic spectrum. They have lived with the condition all their life, unaware of it. This lends weight as to why we would problematize a hard and fast rule around who has authority.

Canadian Ideologies

Earlier, I noted that Carson's mad messiah is a return of some national trauma, likely reflecting on inequality and injustice in contemporary Canada. Does this inequality have to do with the divide between Anglo and Franco communities? In *The Other Quiet Revolution*, Igartua details the ideological framework of an Ontario-centric view of the Canadian nation. Using newspapers of the early period of Canada's history, educational textbooks driven by pivotal change in pedagogical mandates of the sixties, and political commentary on the choosing of the flag in the sixties, Igartua describes a nation organized by its British origins and principles. The impact of this organization is that the quiet revolution in Québec had an equally quiet impact on British English-speaking Canada; in the process of dealing with Québécois unrest, English-speaking Canada slowly divested itself of its authority over the nation, agreeing to share the national identity with Quéebec as exemplified in two official languages. Up until that point, and in some ways, even now, British Canada has defined the French speaking and the first nations as a minority under its rule. In the process of distinguishing itself as a nation in its own right, from Vimy Ridge in World War One to post-World War Two, Canada also found the need to distinguish itself from the influence of the U.S., both politically and culturally, and mainly because of the geographical immediacy of the border. For the most part, Canadian identity took a long time to formalize and even then, Canada's key feature is to be self-effacing, or in McLuhan's terms, lacking identity entirely. Igartua quotes Kieran Kohane's assessment that Canadian identity is "the enjoyment of the endurance of lack of particularity." In other terms, Philip Resnick defines Canada as the "nation that dares not speak its name" (14). Perhaps because Canada seems to erase its identity, it may feel the need to define itself against U.S. culture. This sentiment is proudly expressed in the Molson Canadian commercial "I am Canadian," in which Canada is distinguished negatively against America's stereotype of what a Canadian is. Essentially, it is arguing "I am Canadian because I am not a U.S. citizen because a U.S. citizen has no idea who I am." While this playful commercial seems harmless, the claims about what Canadians are, which does not include the Inuit people, flag the unconscious white settler racism in Canada's "lack of" identity.

It is fascinating to consider how the geography in Carson's work reinforces ideas reflected on by Resnick and Kohane. If Geryon is raised in Canada, the city or nation of his birthplace is never mentioned. The only time geopolitical naming happens is when Geryon travels to study in Buenos Aries, Argentina. When asked "You from the States?" Geryon replies "No" (86) and does not embellish. The irony, of course, is that just as Geryon the beast would not admit his origin is a red island, this red island being ancient and nowhere, so a Canadian would not admit to coming from Canada, it being a nation that is nowhere. Resnick's phrase, "the nation that dares not speak its name," rings loud and clear here.

The lack of particularity draws attention to not seeing the obvious. What is obvious about Canada's identity? In *White Civility*, Coleman associates Canadian identity with British civil culture sustained by white settler citizens who distinguish themselves as Loyalist, unlike the

American rebels. Foreigners, first nations, are all reflected as a minority subjected to the dominant British rule about civility. Coleman notes that the predominant theme in the "nation's self-defining narratives," works of the nineteenth century, is that of the "young maturing man" (40). These narratives are allegorical projects that teach and perform, "what you might call its official and suppressed curriculum—*Žižek* would call these its symbolic and spectral histories" (40). In short, early Canadian literature can be seen as marking imaginary national identities, as per Benedict Anderson's *Imagined Communities*, which are performed through characters in stories that teach Canadians who they are. Canada is defined as a young white man; he is the one with the privilege to be born into civility, marking all the rest of us multicultural fellows as merely "others" that must measure ourselves against him, as lacking and or in need of civilizing.

Coleman sees nationhood as integral to the literary project, and by the twentieth century, the relationship to this civility is compromised by remembering the nation's historical treatment of indigenous peoples, as well as racial minorities. Coleman cites Dennis Lee's poem "Civil Elegies" as exemplifying the Canadian sentiment and the loss of civility. What stands out is how the poem shows a shift away from a positive vision of the future, the progressive quality of history, to a more critical perspective which Coleman calls "wry civility": "Wry civility must also retain self-consciousness about the myth of progress that often subtends the very activity of historical criticism itself." The criticism that Coleman sees in Lee's poetry has a sensibility one would associate with postmodernism. In that sense, we might see "wry civility" in Carson's work, as well. While Carson's mad messiahs do seem to fit the nineteenth century "young maturing man" protagonist, namely Isaiah, Geryon, 4No, among others, they also enable a postmodern critique of progress; fulfillment is always postponed or undermined, time is bent as in Geryon's experience in Argentina, or leaps forward as with 4No's ability to see into the future, and the grand narrative of secular equality is deconstructed. In the hands of a mad messiah, what we have is less world building than a passing through secularism, and troubling it.

It is tempting to see the erasure of Canadian location, or history, in Carson's work as exemplifying what Coleman claims is an attempt to forget the racial violence of the past: "The losses within Canada's civil ideal, the ruptures of racial and other forms of violence that deny the nation's aspirations to become the peaceable kingdom, make up the constitutive losses, which belong within white Canadian settler civility" (34). As such, can we see these messiahs as a return of that violence? In that sense, does the messiah stand as a wish for racial equality? Who is seeking that equality, the white settler or the indigenous person? And what ethnicity or race is her mad messiah if her work is so void of national identity features? Moreover, what traumatic return would be visible in these figures whose features are so generic (prophet) or so fabulous (red winged beast)? Ahead, the task is to look through the symbolic and spectral representation of these mad messiahs and listen for the unconscious messages seeded there about what it means to be Canadian in the late twentieth and early twenty-first centuries.

Suffering Servant

Anne Carson's poetic treatment of the biblical text, "The Book of Isaiah" in her "Book of Isaiah" is an interesting interpretation of the mad messiah, for a few reasons. In Western society, the biblical text has been considered one of the seminal OT prophetic texts of the Christian canon for denoting the coming of Jesus. Early Christian fathers believed the reference to the "suffering servant" (Isaiah 53) confirmed that Jesus, who suffered for the sins of all, was the messiah chosen by God to draw all people to God. For the Jew, the following line reflects the significance of "Isaiah" as defining the exemplarity of the Jewish people: "I will give you as a covenant for the people, a light to the nations" (49: 6). Thus, while the book represents different traditions for each faith, Christianity and Judaism, it also reflects the same promise of inclusion in both faiths. In the pages ahead, I will make a case for seeing Carson's mad messiah as representing a critique of the neurotypical stigma against psychosis. I will also highlight how Carson's secularization of the ancient text may indicate either conscious or unconscious allusions to two historical nineteenth century messiahs, the Métis leader, Louis Riel (1844–85) and the schizophrenic German Judge, Daniel Paul Schreber (1842–1911). In both cases, we can see Carson's postmodern project as undermining secularism and the biblical messiah, but also, in conservative ways, maintaining certain social and political geographies.

Glass, Irony, and God

Scholarship on Carson's work tends to be limited to reviews and to analyses that are focused on her formalistic experiments. Her fusion of fiction, drama, documentary, the essay, with poetry, is characteristic of her experiments, some of which, critics say, are not so good.[8] Complementing the critics' more formalistic interest is a contingent of scholarship focused on her use of mystical ideas, made explicit in her references to Simone Weil and Monica Vitti in *Decreation*, or Isaac the Blind, Teresa d'Avila, and Isaiah in *Glass, Irony and God* not to mention the biblical references interspersed throughout her oeuvre. About *Decreation*, Dan Disney suggests "readers may begin to question whether Carson is writing (as Plato said of all poets) as mad or divinely inspired."[9] The reference to madness and revelation are terms that describe what is being explored most profoundly in "Book of Isaiah," the second last piece of her collection, *Glass, Irony and God*. In his review of many of her texts in the *New York Times Book Reviews*, Charles Simic identifies this "poem" as "a masterful evocation of the visionary rhetoric of Old Testament Prophets." That is all that anyone has said of this poem, to date, and I think it is not enough. Not only is passing praise about the poem not enough, identifying the poem as a "masterful evocation" is problematic, since Carson's work problematizes the master narrative of the Bible along with the religious significance of "evocation." It is instructive to review the biblical material that shows us just how easily the western secular world associates Isaiah with Judaism not from a Jewish perspective, but a Christian one: it is thanks to Second Isaiah that Christian ideology has divine authority.

Isaiah is considered one of the most popular of the prophetic texts for both Christians and Jews; it is also one of the earliest texts that gave

---

8 Charles Simic makes a potentially significant observation about Carson's reflection on genre: "The difficulty I have with Carson is that she labels almost everything she writes as poetry. I don't see the point. We don't care if Beckett's later prose and theater pieces are truly novels, short stories or plays. Whatever they are, they are strong writing. The same is true of Carson" (of "Father's Old Blue Cardigan" in "The Spirit of Play" in *New York Review of Books*, vol 52 no 17 (November 3, 2005). There is also a very interesting public exchange between Solway's criticism of Carson's poetry as over-rated in "The Trouble with Annie" [*Books in Canada* 30.1. July 2001: 24–6] and Ian Rae's excellent rejoinder in "Anne Carson and the Solway Hoaxes," *Canadian Literature*. (Vancouver: Spring 2003, Iss. 176: p. 45).

9 D. Disney "Sublime Disembodiments: Self-as-Other in Anne Carson's *Decreation*." *Orbis Litterarum* [67:1: 2012, 25–38]: 34.

definition to the messianic expectation of the first century A.D. The text is composed of two parts: the first (1–39) is considered written by Isaiah himself in the late eighth century B.C., at some point before or after the Assyrian attack of Hezekiah's palace in the north of Judeah; the second part (40–66), is commonly attributed to Isaiah but since it was written about two hundred years after Isaiah, near the end of the Babylonian exile (sixth century B.C.), and because it was written by another prophet whose name is not known, these chapters are associated with the pseudonym: Second Isaiah.[10] One scholar suggests that the second prophet may have been a woman based on the precedent set by women prophets mentioned in the Torah/OT, such as Miriam and Deborah and Hudah.

The interpretation of this prophetic text differs for Jews and Christians. Jewish scholars are divided about who Isaiah was referencing when identifying the "suffering servant." Some suggest that Isaiah was reflecting on a historical figure in the Israelite past; others suggest Isaiah was referencing himself as the suffering "chosen one"; more contemporary interpretations see the "suffering servant" as pointing to all the people of the Nation of Israel, identified at times in the chapters as Zion. The Christians hold to the tradition that Isaiah's reference to the "suffering servant" was a prophetic work about the coming of Jesus Christ. Deutero-Isaiah is the source for the famous concept of the "suffering servant" (Isaiah 53) that has been associated with Jesus' suffering on the cross. What is interesting is to recognize that what we hear today as predetermined, linking Isaiah to Jesus, was in fact a process that happened over several centuries involving extensive revisions of the so-called biblical promise to fit the facts of the historical Jesus.

In the Gospel of Mark, the oldest text of the NT and written in the latter half of the first century A.D.,[11] we read an allusion to the "suffering servant" in the following lines that, make no mention of the cross which suggests the cross association was invented after Mark: "For even

---

10 Of this second part, scholars suggest that there was yet another author of the Chapters 54–66, known as titro-Isaiah.

11 The dating of this ancient text is based on Mark 13:2 which references the destruction of the Second Temple (70 A.D.) that was a critical event in the middle of the Jewish Wars from 66 to 74 A.D. The Gospel was most likely written after the event, barring evidence that this reference was included after the Gospel had been written.

the Son of Man came not to be served, but to serve and to give" (Mark 10:45). While there is no direct reference to "suffering," the reflection on "to serve" alludes to the Deutero-Isaiah phrase. Paul of Tarsus' letters, predating Mark by some decades, includes many references to Isaiah, and notably cites Deutero-Isaiah (40–66) 24 times in one of his last letters, which was to the Romans in 57 A.D. As I have argued in detail in my monograph, *Secular Messiahs*, those references are not necessarily about Jesus but, in fact, more often than not, are about Paul, himself, as a means of justifying his authority as an Apostle to the Gentiles. Since his mission was fulfilling Isaiah's prophecy about Israel being a "light unto the nations," Paul could position himself as the legitimate apostle of Jesus; even though he never knew the living Jesus, he was acting as a "light unto the nations" by attracting converts.

Comparing Carson's representation of the messianic Isaiah to the ancient Israelite text can shed light on the role secular ideology plays in obscuring Christian ideology in secularism. That is, the questions we could ask are: does her work reinstate the secular critique of religion? And if it does, does her work ultimately affirm Anidjar's claims that secularism is a false religiously "neutral" system? By way of not being coy, I admit here that it will be obvious that Carson tends to maintain a Christo-centric narrative in this long poem, which not only upholds secularism, but also attests to a Christo-centric interpretation of Isaiah. This is probably unconscious, as the historical conflict between Judaism and Christianity in this particular biblical text is not common knowledge. In fact, the Christian narrative in Isaiah has operated as a kind of benchmark of fact: Jesus was foretold in the Old Testament. Finally, Carson's work tends to be centered not on a static "any" subject, nor even a particularly male subject, but rather, a subject that one would say, in psychoanalytic terms, is psychotic. But this psychotic subject is not created in a vacuum: there happen to be significant figures in European and Canadian history that consciously or unconsciously have likely informed Carson's postmodern representation of Isaiah. That historical influence shall be a part of the discussion, ahead.

Carson's Book of Isaiah

Her long poem is made of up four parts, loosely defining a narrative of the relationship between God and the Nation of Israel, through God's relationship to Isaiah. Carson secularizes key biblical concepts such as "sin" as a name for the pain of love (107) and the biblical covenant for "contract." Carson's God offers a new twist on the biblical God, portrayed as terrifying not because of his grandeur, but because he is so mercurial and cruel. God makes Isaiah wake anxious because he was "filling [Isaiah's] ears with stingers" (107). God's cruelty, far from having biblical proportions, is ironically converted into minor and even impossible affects. He "shattered Isaiah's indifference" and "smashed Isaiah like glass through every socket of his nation" (108). God's cruelty is compounded by how he manages to manipulate Isaiah to accept the latest "contract" and take on more and more responsibilities. For example, God gives Isaiah a vision of animals tortured by fire, in order to convince Isaiah to "save" the animals (114). In short, God is driven by the kind of punishing cruelty we associate with the divine figure of the Old Testament.

It is obvious that there is nothing loving in this God. That lack of love is not about God's indifference, but about "his" complicated human psychology. As well as having supernatural powers, this God has a body that sweats and cries (115). In this sense, we can see an influence of the Greek gods on Carson's work to secularize the biblical force in line with Ludwig Feuerbach's perceptive psychological proposition that our divine figure is simply a delusion. According to Feuerbach, since God was a project of man himself, the way to liberate mankind from the delusion was to assume the role of God: by making God human, one takes on God's creative power. In this creation, specifically, Carson honors the source of the Old Testament God, giving a little Greek spin to the "brim and fury" by representing her creation as irrational and selfish as Zeus.

As per Feuerbach, this is a postmodern project that self-consciously acknowledges that the God of Isaiah, in this poem, is not divine, and that divine messages do not come from God, but from the people. For example, in Isaiah's speech to the nation about the *camera obscura* and the pinhole created in a darkened room, he says: "You can hold anything up in front of that pinhole, said Isaiah, and worship it on the opposite wall" (111). The nation replies "Why worship an image?" This question reflects the Old Testament God's commandment against idolatry not from God's perspective, but from the human perspective. Notice that in this secular revision, a Protestant asceticism is reflected in this critique of "graven images": the Protestant faith avoids the saints, drawing from Luther's criticism of Catholic indulgences: one cannot buy access to heaven, nor lobby a saint on one's behalf. The only path to heaven is "The Holy Book" and communion with the divine. It is worth emphasizing that Carson's Isaiah has a direct line to the divine through God's word that follows the biblical text closely. This would suggest that, while on the surface Isaiah's God is a secularization of the Old Testament figure, it is substantially expressing an unconscious debt to Protestantism which points to the WASP ruling class both in the United States and in Canada and their faith in The Book. Something to bear in mind is that this representation of Isaiah seems not to distinguish between Canadian and U.S. cultures.

Isaiah is no more than a man of our modern time, with physical and spiritual weaknesses, evident in taking seriously God's cruelties. God seems far from divine, represented as a "not all-knowing" figure since, after he smashes Isaiah in "all his sockets," he accuses Isaiah of lying. "Isaiah is a small man, said Isaiah, but no liar" (109) which is to say that the all-knowing God would know Isaiah is innocent: Carson's God does not. In the biblical text, Isaiah is known as a man who does not lie, though God persecutes him and blames him for the sins of humankind: "And the Lord visited upon him/ the guilt of all of us. / Though he had done no injustice/ And had spoken no falsehood" (53: 8–9). What distinguishes the biblical Isaiah in his suffering from Carson's Isaiah is not his being the victim of an unfair attack, but that he is completely blameless. The biblical God knows he is blameless; Carson's God does not. It seems that Carson inverts this tiny detail of the lie from biblical Isaiah in order to undermine the divine narrative of God's authority, which in turn, maintains the secular investment in society as homo-centric.

Isaiah undergoes a transformation from prophet to messiah half-way through the long poem. Seeing Isaiah as another Jesus is promoted by the metonymic feature of the "Branch." The Branch first appears in Part I as the simple fauna of Isaiah's world, the place under which he and God speak ("They conversed under the Branch," 107). In Part II, as Isaiah's suffering increases, ("A Burden was upon Isaiah," 111), "the sigh grew into a howl/ the howl ran along brooks …" (112), driving him to leave. He "walked for three years." This "retreat" takes on a symbolic value when he becomes "the Branch roaming against the sky like a soul" (112). Perhaps because of the loose allusion to St. John of the Cross's "dark night of the soul" here, one our western culture cannot "unsee," there is a troubling of that Christian narrative through the ironic and literal rendering of Isaiah's equivalence to Jesus in the metaphor of the "Branch."

Carson's "Branch" draws on a biblical reference to Jesus's messianic legitimacy as the descendant of King David. In the first century A.D., the "messiah" was a loose principle, and open for interpretation, and one of the lines of interpretation was the Bible. So the Gospels documented the connections. For example, in Matthew 1:1–17, Jesus's lineage, through his mother, connects him to King David, the first example of the "mesiach" (Hebrew for chosen), the king chosen by God. This idea that King David's offspring would lead the Judeans in a future victory was grounded in interpretations of Isaiah. In First Isaiah, we read how Israel would have a new King David, signaled by his other name, "Jesse": "But a shoot shall grow out of the stump of Jesse,/ A twig shall sprout from his stock" (11:1). In Second Isaiah, and specifically in the opening lines of Isaiah 53, the "Branch" metaphor as an allusion to offspring of King David becomes more pronounced: "For he was grown, by His favor, like a tree crown, like a tree trunk out of arid ground" (53: 2). In the biblical "Isaiah," the association between David and the coming messiah as the "offshoot" of a tree, or "Branch," was central to justifying Jesus's messianic status. He was the "suffering servant" that we read of in the biblical text. Thus, Carson's Isaiah is a Jesus figure: he is marked by the symbol of his lineage and yet, this "lineage" is not the "blood line" or "right of blood" that is integral to Matthew, but to a more inclusive notion of "humanity," a secular project of social justice for all. Isaiah is the "everyman." Ironically, Carson's Isaiah "being marked" is a postmodern deconstruction of the Christian resurrection narrative which reinforces the failure of secularism to fulfill its promise of equality.

Carson's Isaiah shows an amazingly vivid connection to the story of Louis Riel, the Métis messianic leader who was tried and convicted for treason for his part in instigating two Rebellions (1870 and 1885). Riel was deemed mad by his lawyers in order to save him from being executed. Riel resisted this definition. Isaiah has been rendered mad in Carson's work. Riel's lawyers render Riel mad.

Is this claim to madness a lie? In that sense, is Riel's action the historical source for Carson's focus on Isaiah's lie? According to Gregory Betts who wrote about Riel's legal team's effort to find him not guilty of treason because of insanity, the Métis leaders' tendency to pray in the nude signaled to some that he was not sane. But was this way of praying simply not biblical? Betts asks: "Isaiah, for instance, wanders the world for three years in the nude under God's direct instruction (Isaiah 20:2)" (29). Do we go too far in speculating here that Carson's Isaiah seems modeled on Riel? Where Isaiah wandered "under a Branch" for three years, Riel prayed in the nude for three years. Where Carson's Isaiah was a prophet turned messiah, Riel, the "Prophet of the New World" was also a messiah who was "devoted to healing the Protestant-Catholic rift in the Christian church and to his belief in the Métis as a chosen people" (26). We might even see God's treatment of Isaiah in Carson's poem as paralleled by the way the Canadian government "permanently silenced" Riel with execution (28). Drawing an association between Carson's Isaiah and Louis Riel is purely speculative and may be considered by some to be "scarcely probable," but a connection may be made if we consider that Riel is recognized as a Canadian messiah. Moreover, seeing an equation between this history of Canada's abysmal treatment of the Métis peoples and God's abusive treatment of Isaiah in Carson's work would be interesting. Besides that, Riel's story was in the cultural *zeitgeist* at the time that Carson was writing her long poem: in 1982, the Canadian government granted status to Métis people, and by 1998, the Canadian government honored Riel's legacy by formally apologizing for his execution. Why not see Carson's Isaiah as an allusion to Riel?

If we see an allusion to a first nations figure in Carson's Isaiah, that would mean Carson's messiah is Métis. Can we see in Carson's poem a "mad anti-colonial challenge to the extension of the Dominion of Canada across the north-West" (Betts 22)? Considering Carson's Isaiah stands out as a savior in a world of animals, a landscape in which there are so few people, we might see a small insult to the great Métis leader who had a strong and loyal following. As well, Carson's Isaiah is, as already determined, not Catholic, like Riel, but secular. Nor is he executed for treason, a detail which no Canadian should leave unaddressed in a portrayal of Riel. Finally, Isaiah is represented as mad whereas, as Betts's points out, Riel's madness is a historical question. This is all to propose that the strongest association we can read between the Métis leader and Carson's biblical prophet may be considered an unconscious one, indicating a historical trauma. This analysis is speculative by nature: it may apply in part, in whole, or not at all, but the possibility is one worth considering. As it stands, since Isaiah may be considered a Christian, not Jewish, figure in Carson's work, we may say that Riel, or the history he represents, returns in Carson's Isaiah to signify the trauma of the Canadian government's abusive treatment of the Métis people, the unfair conviction and execution of Riel in the greater context of Canada's violence against and mistreatment of indigenous peoples. In that sense, Carson's Isaiah may be considered the return of the trauma of white settler's unconscious guilt.

Between Part III and Part IV, Carson's Isaiah undergoes a transformation that fuses the biblical Israelite prophet with the Christian messiah. Isaiah endures a "night," full of the "roar" of silence (113) and then is given the vision of fire on the back of a deer: "Isaiah saw the deer of the nation burning all along its back" (114); an animal representing the nation, "turned/ until its shadow lay tangled around its feet like melted wings." Interestingly, Carson exploits the imagery found in the biblical Second Isaiah, but completely revises the message of the prophet. Second Isaiah is speaking to the people, explaining how "the Lord God gave me a skilled tongue ... The Lord God opened my ears" (50-4-5) to send the message that those who do not follow the Lord will suffer: "But you are all kindlers of fire, Girding on firebrands. Walk by the blaze of your fire, By the brands that you have lit. This has come to you from my hand; You shall lie down in pain" (50: 11). Whereas Second Isaiah is the one speaking, and creating the imagery that can warn the people to avoid their suffering, Carson's Isaiah is receiving the image from God and it is torture; God tortures Isaiah. This vision is God's last manipulative move to have Isaiah accept the responsibility of saving "the nation," leading to the continuation of the "contract" (115).

But Isaiah's ultimate transformation is becoming female which links Carson's Isaiah with another historical messiah: namely, Daniel Paul Schreber. In Second Isaiah, we read the dialogue between "Zion" or the Judeans and God, where the former complains that "The Lord has forsaken me" and God self-identifies as a woman: "Can a woman forget her baby, Or disown the child of her womb? Though she might forget, I never could forget you" (49:15). As creator, God is mother and more than mother, signaling the superior status of the inhuman creator over the mere human. In Carson's long poem, Isaiah takes on this divine status, changing into a woman through the letting down of milk: "It was a silk and bitter sensation" (117), that signals what God calls a "new contract!" Whereas the inhuman God can nurture and care for the inferior human, so the human Isaiah can nurture and care for an inferior class, namely animals: "As he fed the milk to small birds and animals Isaiah thought only about their little lips" (117). Notable is that the hierarchy from God down to man down to animal is being manipulated by Carson for her project. Birds don't have lips, which shifts the irony here into a zone of the fabulous. How reliable is this Isaiah if impossible visions keep interfering in his reality? For that matter, is Isaiah mad? And in that question, the hierarchy that puts humans above animals falls apart.

When the secularized Isaiah converses with God, we are seeing this prophetic narrative through the science of psychoanalysis; a psychotic's delusion that God is talking to him. In psychoanalytic terms, Isaiah is not a prophet, but a man suffering auditory and visual hallucinations. Isaiah is not an actual woman, equal in some measure to God's creative class, nor should we mistake him for the "savior" that was Jesus, since Jesus in the Christian tradition, was divine. Rather, Carson's Isaiah appears more like Daniel Paul Schreber, the first diagnosed Paranoid Schizophrenic. He was a German Judge of the nineteenth century who documented his psychotic episodes and his life while incarcerated in a mental institute in his *Memoirs of My Nervous Illness* (1910). Schreber's delusions were several, but the one that is primary is that he believed that he was a messiah, being transformed into a woman to save the world.

Schreber's psychosis was apparent in his megalomania (belief that he was the messiah) and in the fact that instead of one God, he had two Gods speaking to him: they singled him out for their enjoyment, naming him "wretch," overwhelming him with "nerve language," and changing him into a wife. Schreber believed he was undergoing a sex change evident in the feminizing of his body; only once his transformation was completed, would he be able to save mankind. His physiological transformation, he argued, was in his developing breasts and hips; to accentuate this change, he began dressing himself in ribbons. This gender change experienced by Schreber is not very far off from Carson's representation of Isaiah's experiences. As Schreber was persecuted by his Gods, so Isaiah is persecuted by God and treated like a "wretch." He is feminized for his savior powers: he wakes with a "sensation below the neck, it was silk and bitter sensation." Then from his breasts milk "pour[ed] like strings" to feed the nations. Notable is how Isaiah's milk seems to emulate Schreber's ribbons as both "silk" and "strings." We may speculate that Carson's Isaiah not only secularizes the biblical text, it also renders a poetic representation of Schreber's schizophrenic experiences. Is Carson conscious of the association between Schreber and her Isaiah in a way that she may not be in the connection I showed between Riel and her Isaiah? That we cannot say, but seeing both figures in Isaiah is encouraged by the details of the text.

In contemporary terms, we see Isaiah's sex change manifesting a queer politics, of sorts, representative of Schreber's homosexuality. Where the politics wavers, or is incomplete, is in the fact that Isaiah's sex change ends when he reverts to his masculine self. After changing back into a man, Isaiah knows "several wives" and begets "a bastard son," returning us very much to The Bible's misogynist narrative. Meanwhile, at night, he remembers his feminine self: "his dreams slipped a river of milk." So, in the day he is a man and at night, a woman; through time, he balances his male and female selves: "prophecies continued to feature *eunuch cylinders* and *clickfoot woman shame*" during the day, while in his dreams the miracle of his sexual change haunts him. In other words, Isaiah, the mad messiah, the one possibly modeled on Schreber and Riel, both, embodies the postmodern deconstruction of Jesus, the Christian messiah.

An interesting reflection on Carson's westernizing of Isaiah may gesture to a particular Canadian quality to the story. The Nation of Israel is a kind of veil for any nation; the deer is a kind of westernizing of the Asian antelope, the gazelle. In other words, Carson has translated the narrative as happening anywhere in the west. The poem's social geography appears generic. But remember that generic tends to be the Canadian poet's code for Canada ("A nation that dares not speak its name"). Moreover, Carson's reinvention of the biblical Hebrew tradition into contemporary Canadian/ American English, may be seen as a colonization of the biblical material—or, in the Christian sense, a successionist revision. As already noted, Isaiah would likely not consciously be Métis, but unconsciously the figure may point to a white settler guilt. That whiteness may be seen as sustained by Schreber, a white European subject. This white representation of the ancient biblical figure has a precedent in European representations of Jesus: he is generally depicted as a fair haired and blue-eyed man. The critique of graven images I argue indicates a Protestant faith over a Catholic faith and unconsciously represents the British imperialist dominion that Igartua associated with Canada's ruling Anglo-centric (Anglican/Protestant) class. Moreover, since it is a colonizer's project, any Métis in Isaiah has been subsumed by colonial guilt. This you could say is the trauma represented in this mad messiah: a historical fact of inequality in Canadian society. In one respect, Carson's Isaiah may break down the secular master narrative by gesturing to some politics, a wish to show equality to the queer and or Métis subject, while all it does is fortify the elitism of the white Anglo-Saxon Protestant settler rule.

Conclusion

If Carson's Isaiah was probably meant to show an equality between Judaism and Christianity and man and woman, was it also trying to reflect on the equality between indigenous and settler peoples in Canada? Carson's Isaiah is a secular project which means it is not religiously neutral. In fact, it promotes Christian salvation that, I have suggested, indicates a Protestantism that we could say denotes both the Canadian and American founding fathers. Since Canada's ruling elite mirrors in so many ways the ruling elite of the United States, what could signify this Isaiah as Canadian? I would say that what distinguishes Canada from the United States is the Canadian treatment of indigenous peoples as apparent in the story of Louis Riel. Seeing a Riel narrative driving the Isaiah messiah could indicate an unconscious and deeply buried return of the trauma of Canada's policies and acts of violence against the First Nations peoples. Whereas Isaiah may have tried to liberate mankind from the masculine gender and include women in messianic practice, and whereas Riel tried in his life to liberate the Métis people from the Canadian government's oppressive treatment, Carson's secularized Isaiah is a Christian paradigm of liberation which, as a true postmodern anti-hero, does not succeed in liberating anyone. In fact, Carson's postmodern critique of the master narrative of messianic redemption leaves the ruling elite of white secular settlers intact, indicating how stubborn colonialism is, and how vulnerable indigenous people are in Canada. If we can see Riel in Isaiah, then Carson's Isaiah is a Canadian messiah. Instead of being Catholic like Riel, Isaiah is Protestant like Canada's ruling class.

I will end with an acknowledgment that Carson's treatment of psychosis in the biblical narrative is where her poem achieves something momentous: as a postmodern project, it deconstructs a master narrative of madness. The social expectations are that people in psychosis are a burden on society. In reality, Schreber was a burden to his wife which is why she had him institutionalized; Riel was a burden on Canadian society both as a rebel and as a putative madman. If we consider that madness is not a liability but a gift of revelation, that messianic figures in history are figures who have been called by some higher order for political intervention, then the contrast between the long history of revelation and the present conditions of treatment of psychosis, stands out vividly. The fact Carson exposes that master narrative of madness as faulty, that she is questioning the neurotypical judgment of psychosis as an abnormality, means that she is supporting a Mad Studies critique. But whether Carson is doing so as someone who is on the spectrum, as would be supported by Mad Studies scholars, is not something I can address in this chapter, but will in the next.

CHAPTER 3

Geryon, Resurrected

Introduction

The autistic subject, as with the schizophrenic, is on the psychotic spectrum. A strictly Jamesonian analysis of autistic representation as a messianic figure is somewhat thwarted by the fact that, in the cultural tradition, the autist is not a liberating figure. Rather it is seen as a condition of weakness that requires a cure. Works such as *Rainman* exemplify a general anxiety about those with this condition. Anne Carson's *Autobiography of Red* is in many ways a project similar to the Hollywood version, with a significant exception: it takes an ambivalent approach to the need for a "cure." The protagonist, Geryon, an ancient Greek red beast who had been killed by Herakles centuries ago, is resurrected for this novel as a queer autistic subject. The implication of this resurrection is that he is on par with Jesus, and in that sense, has a messianic vocation. In the opening chapters, we see Geryon is, as a boy, at the mercy of the world around him, until he starts building an autobiography with photos. This photographic process allows him to bridge his eternal self, a Jesus figure, with his autistic self, the temporal secular subject: because of this power, he does not die after his encounter with Herakles; because of it, he is able to share "immortality" with his colleagues. The narrative offers a cure that does not erase his madness and in this way Geryon, the mad messiah, is liberated and liberating.

The analysis ahead is concerned with exploring the dialogue, or relationship, between the neurotypical elements of this project, the autobiography as narrative, and the neurodivergent elements, Geryon's character and actions, to define this mad messiah and the unconscious cultural matter informing it. Moreover, I am interested in determining: first, to what extent Mad Studies can criticize postmodern representations of the psychotic subject; and second, if we can determine a Canadian trauma in this mad messiah.

Against the Cure

According to Lacan, there are three registers of psychic life: the imaginary, the symbolic and the real. The imaginary points to the illusive quality of one's identity, self-image. The symbolic defines all systems we live with from language to math to architecture to governments and the laws we live by. Meanwhile, the real is the ineffable, inexplicable and sometimes horrifying force that affects us when we least expect it. This is why Lacan says that trauma is the subject's encounter with the real. As a result of this encounter, the subject builds a "fantasy" that organizes the trauma, while the reason that the fantasy manifests in so many different forms is because it is built from the remainder of the encounter which is called the *objet a*. This residue is so immaterial it has been defined by *Žižek* as the "hole at the center of the symbolic." An Oedipalized subject is one who lives with the symbolic, manipulates it well, because they have accepted the rule of law in the Name of the Father (NOF). With the symbolic, they can organize their trauma by building up a fantasy or narrative.

The autist is signified by the One who forecloses the NOF and has no Other or object. The foreclosure manifests in an a-sociality and a resistance to symbolic systems such as language. The autist is disarmingly self-absorbed, which Lacan explains reflects her immersion in the imaginary without the symbolic tools to interpret it: "As the name indicates, autistic children hear themselves. They hear many things. This even ends up normally in hallucination, and the hallucination always has a more or less vocal character" (Tendlarz 16). Yasmin Gasser articulates the autist's inability to grasp the symbolic function of language to the extent that it can lead to the infant's inability to demand food:

"Autism's weight of words corresponds [...] to a serious slowing down of language serial games."[12] These are descriptions of autistic subjects on the extreme end of the spectrum. For those that partially socialize, such as high functioning autists, what remains a key feature of the condition is the inability to recognize metaphor as representation; they tend to take language statements literally; they have trouble manipulating the symbolic.[13] Notable about these assessments of autism is that the condition is considered a deviation from the Oedipalized norm. Meanwhile, the Oedipal world is hard pressed to develop methods to convert the autistic subject to the Oedipal side.

In reaction to the growing attention by parents and healthcare professionals to cure autists of their condition, E. L. Bragg's video *In My Language* (2007) on Youtube, testifies to the value of autistic life. Divided into two parts, the first half of the video is composed of static framed shots of Braggs fiddling with objects, moving her hands and arms as if flying. The second half, titled "A Translation," introduces a computerized voice-over that is meant to "translate" the visual collage of her motion which "is about being in a constant conversation with every part of my environment," she explains. Her translation, the language used to explain what we are looking at, retroactively signifies for us that, what we saw as aimless activity, is actually a meaningful dialogue with her surroundings, in sensual, non-symbolic terms. That is, when she says that we should not read the water symbolically while watching water from the tap run onto her hands, she wants to stress that what we read imagisticly in the video is, for her, evidence of the foreclosure of the NOF because it is a purely sensory experience; the word "water" literally means her experience of flowing wet. Even these words do not do justice to her experience.

What is striking about Braggs' video is that the computer-generated voice with which she asks us not to see the water as symbolizing something, has for us an alien and alienating quality, which works metaphorically for us to grasp the distance between what we understand about

12 This quote by Yasmin Grasser "The Weight of Words," translated by Jorge Jauregui. *Lacanian Ink 1*, (1990) Web. The auditory nature of the psychotic's hallucinations is discussed by Lacan in "On the Question Prior to Any Possible Treatment of Psychosis" (*Écrits* 446).

13 It has to be noted that these generalizations do not fairly depict the differences among people on the spectrum.

her and who she is. In conveying the truth of her life for us Oedipalized audiences, she is using the very symbolic order she forecloses as an autist, verifying that the autistic subject is not without an ability to use the symbolic order and mostly, that her autistic relation to the *real* eludes us. We are witnessing her struggle with harnessing the symbolic to "mean" her experiences and what we hear in this computerized voice is her discomfort with meaning; all that we can access of her is her compromised relation to the symbolic, which is the inversion of her experience of the *real* ecstasy, where she remains free of the symbolic that grips us, her neurotypical viewer. Even my interpretation of her discomfort does her a disservice in that it symbolizes her experience through meaning. These layers of signification and resistance to signification in Bragg's work help to frame how we might read *Autobiography*.

In comparison to Braggs' experience, Anne Carson's *Autobiography* looks less like an autistic representation by an autist than an autistic representation by a neurotypical subject. Yet, it is not a Hollywood representation of an autistic life either, since it indicates a similar discomfort of the conditions of living that Braggs' expresses. Carson's text is not like Braggs' autobiography; whereas Braggs makes the case that she needs neither pity nor cure, *Autobiography* represents a protagonist for whom we feel pity for his discomfort which leads to being satisfied in seeing the healing energy of the metaphorical cure: photography. If Braggs' text can be seen literally as the trauma of the symbolic, which intersects the real, the trauma of Carson's *Autobiography* is the cure, or the assimilation/integration of the autistic exception into the social fold.

In the interview with di Michele, Carson contends that "genres are conventional" and "Conventions exist to be renegotiated." This defines a creative approach that serves the interest of this project for exploring a "general textuality." Her experiments with prose and poetry through secularizing mystical sources exemplified in her first publication, the series of prose poems, *Short Talks* (1992), recurs as experiments with generic structures in all her subsequent works. *Autobiography* is no different: it announces its experiment as a fusion of the narrative of "fiction" with the metaphorical power of "verse" through recreating the autobiography of the mythic winged beast named Geryon. He is a "monster," the winged-figure named Geryon who, in Greek mythology, was killed by the half-mortal, Herakles, and his biography is found in the extant ancient Greek fragments of Stesichoros. As we read Carson's argument that Stesichoros's story is important because it tells about Herakles from the perspective of the monster he killed (Geryon), we are alerted to a new subjectivity in Carson's figure. The beast is resurrected as a Greco-Jesus autistic subject: he is a mad messiah.

It is worth considering the significance of the features of Geryon's difference. He is red. He considers himself a monster. He is autistic and as we come to understand, gay. These stigmas in the social order, that explain his identification with being a "beast," are central to Carson's postmodernist project. She is deconstructing the heteronormative neurotypical master narratives. But his redness stands out as purely abstract. In the Canadian context, can we see in Geryon's redness an identification with the indigenous subject? I would say "no" for several reasons. For one, the cultural references of the beast are entirely western-centric. Since Geryon is an ancient Greek mythic figure, and ancient Greece is the birthplace of western culture, his "redness' is already culturally associated with a settler's sensibility; it is not equated with North American indigeneity. In fact, to see a racial essentializing of the indigenous people in Geryon would involve colonizing the First Nations peoples in literary terms, and *Autobiography* does not seem to go in that direction. Moreover, the color red becomes associated with the green of grass (24), which suggests the color is either arbitrary or associated with territory (i.e. Nation). Finally, Geryon's community appears generically middle class, which suggests Geryon is ethnically of the dominant colonial culture. In other words, he would be considered a white settler. Geryon's redness may simply be the signifier for his autism and his homosexuality.

Seeing Geryon as white settler is encouraged if we see Geryon as a representation of Carson. Carson encourages us to see this connection through her allusion to Gertrude Stein's experimental *Autobiography of Alice B. Toklas*. If Stein's testimony hides the truth of her masculine-like authority and lesbian love in a fictional Alice B. Toklas self-telling while creating a representation of herself through a fictional collaboration with her "other," we are encouraged to recognize that Geryon is a reflection of Carson about herself. But really: is this Anne Carson's autobiography, much in the way we read Toklas' autobiography as Stein's self-telling? Sharno Wahl makes the argument that yes, Geryon's story is probably littered with Carson's story. For example, in high school, Carson used to dress up as Oscar Wilde, signifying what can be seen as an identification with Geryon's queer subjectivity. If the autobiography of *Autobiography* may be Anne Carson's reflexive self-telling through the "fictional other" of Geryon, that personal story raises questions about why Carson resurrects the primordial mythic monster as herself? Is the autistic child a beast who, even after growing into a socialized young man, remains an autist? Is there a wry Steinian confession happening here? We can consider addressing this in the conclusion.

We are introduced to Geryon on the first day of school traumatized by his condition of synesthesia, hearing sound in color. Synesthesia is a phenomenological condition of early life, as noted by Merleau-Ponty: "our primordial experience in the lifeworld is synesthetic experience, a natural commingling of the senses". With respect to primordial, it is clear that we are in a pre-Oedipal stage known as the mirror stage which is associated with a child's early development: the child, on seeing themselves in the mirror as a single defined body, achieves some independence. It is not until the infant has passed through the Oedipal stage, that they can see they exist in a community, the most immediate community being the family, and all senses start to become defined: red is different from green. The mirror stage, in most psychoanalytic circles, is where the autistic subject remains, unwilling to accept the NOF. The color Geryon hears most deeply is red, the color with which he identifies himself. His condition leads him to experience "red" as sound and, as seen in the following passage, as smell: "He was focusing hard on his feet and his steps./ Children poured around him/ and the intolerable red assault of grass and the smell of grass everywhere/ was pulling him towards it" (*Autobiography* 23). Note that in seeing grass as "red," Geryon's color-blindness makes "red" not "red," a detail I suggest expresses the autist's troubled relation to language.

Geryon's physical reality is a confusion of what can be identified as hallucinatory experiences: color is noise and people are currents and smell exerts a force on him. The poetic nature of Carson's text amplifies the instability of his environment and social reality. Telescoping of details anchors the boy against the anxiety induced by the liquidity of children on his first day of school, but creates that self-focused attention at the exclusion of exterior stimuli. The boy's hallucinatory sensory overload, perhaps similar to Braggs' sensory life, is exacerbated when his brother abandons him, sending him into crisis: "the world dropped away" and what would have served as a map to help him get into the school was void of symbolization as a "deep glowing blank" (24). Geryon's social isolation is compounded by the fact that he has the linguistic troubles Gasser defines as the "weight of words": "The words each blew towards him and came apart on the wind" (26). Geryon's first experience of society, our first view of him, represents his being caught by the real without the symbolic order to help navigate. In effect, we feel some anxiety to protect Geryon.

The cure for autism is evident in Klein's seminal research on autistic children and her famous case study with a boy named Dick. In therapy sessions, when Dick played with toys, Klein understood that the toy train was for Dick literally a train. Through play therapy, Klein was able to teach Dick to transfer symbolic significance to the toy; that is, once he was able to see himself as the train, he was then able to perform subsequent symbolic associations, such as seeing his mother as the "station." This working through of symbolic meaning "cured" Dick of his "separation anxieties" that had inhibited socialization. In Lacanian terms, Dick's recognition of the train's metaphorical trick indicated his Oedipalization; that is, Dick began to see his mother as replaceable through playing with toys: thus, he was able to organize his world through symbolic systems. Klein's "cure" models what the narrator does in *Autobiography*: just as Klein rehabilitates Dick with games, so the narrator Oedipalizes Geryon with photographs.

Geryon's cure is a kind of therapeutic intervention in autobiographical representation. Where Braggs resists Oedipalization, Geryon's autobiography embraces it through his photographic diary: "he set down all inside things/ particularly his own heroism ... he coolly omitted/ all outside things" (29). Clearly, in identifying the inside from outside and demarcating the field of omission, a procedure central to the NOF has occurred; he has organized his world between himself and the Other. If Geryon, the autistic character, is domain of "inside things" of the *real*, he will, through the course of the novel be aided in organizing the outside world through photographs which we grasp by the narrator's representation. Through the third person, the narrator provides Geryon with the symbolic order, required to be "other" to himself.

The autist's tendency to see "everything symbolic become *real*" ("Autistic Children", Sylvia Tendlarz 13), is expressed in the photos. Cultural scholar Stuart Murray suggests that in the novella the photo is "Geryon's fetish of choice" ("The Autobiographical Self: Phenomenology and the Limits of Self-Possession" 114). I would argue that seeing the photographs as "fetish" does not do justice to what the photos are accomplishing, for the character and the novel's plot; moreover, "fetish" is a term that would be applied to a fully Oedipalized subject which does not describe Geryon in this initial period of the representation. I would argue for seeing the photo as the metaphors organizing his life. Technically, the photo demands neither verbal processing nor even an interest in the metaphorical function of representation to initiate. Geryon's photos are equivalent to the video representation of Braggs' touching water, her literal piece of reality. Our digesting of her experience in representation does not disturb her experience with water. In essence, the photos allow Geryon to remain safe in his autism. This you could say is the principle behind separating inside from outside things.

The photographs exploit the relationship between the literal and metaphorical, expressed in the title given to the photo and the context for the photo. For example, the title, "It is a close-up photograph of Geryon's left leg just below the knee" (*Autobiography* 137) is literally what the photo is of. It is the narrator's explanation of what was happening when the photo was taken, the context, that provides the metaphorical significance. The metaphorical significance is about danger. The photo was taken accidentally when Ancash's mother shoved Geryon's camera down and out of sight of the soldiers who had suddenly appeared. The presence of soldiers signifies a military state or a contested border where a camera is the tool for a spy or a journalist to disguise themselves as an innocent tourist. Someone with a camera could inspire a soldier to shoot. For Geryon, the photo is literally an accidental shot of his leg; for the reader, it represents a metaphorical wound standing for what did not happen since Ancash's mother saved Geryon by shoving his camera out of sight. In the narrator's hands, this photo is the occasion of the ironic accidental *tuché*. But it also immortalizes Geryon. Literally, the photo has a material life longer than human, much as Stesichoro's fragments hold the story of Geryon's life over the centuries.

E. L. McCallum makes an interesting argument that the *punctum*—that moment which disappears in the flash of the shutter—represents the traumatic moment of forgetting (par. 12 and II, par. 43). Drawing on Roland Barthe's theory of the punctum in photography, McCallum contextualizes Carson's literary innovation: "the synesthetic power of the *punctum*, thus, is central to what Carson brings to a theory of photography" (II par. 28). The fact that the *punctum* signifies a trauma of forgetting at the heart of photographic representation is not only a powerful critique of modern technology as a device for psychic interventions, in my analysis it also serves to show how Geryon's camera functions much like Braggs' computer-generated voice; it Oedipalizes the subject while freeing the subject from Oedipalization. For the autistic Geryon, who has "progressed" to the symbolic through the holophrasis of the photo, the *punctum* and its non-verbal, pure sensory flash, do the impossible by leaving the autist's *real* inassimilable. Without the narrator/author's role in framing the *punctum* as a photograph retroactively with a title and an explanation of how the photo came to be taken, there would be no autobiography or story; without the narrator's voice, Geryon's immortality would be missed. In effect, the narrator enables a "cure" that protects Geryon from surrendering to the NOF.

Immortality

Geryon's photography is not simply a device to convert the autist's madness in a way the neurotypical audience can understand; rather, and more importantly, it is a device which establishes Geryon's special relation to the eternal real of his messianic status. I would argue that what McCallum identifies as the camera's apotropaic function (McCallum II par. 22) is a powerful concept in recognizing its significance for Geryon, the autist. The magic of his photos is not just indicated by technology's ability to make a print of reality, but is reflected in the photograph's ability to represent the autistic figure as a resurrected subject: it literalizes the symbolic order as it immortalizes Geryon. The fusing of temporal reality of autism with Geryon's eternity plays out as the messianic power of resurrection.

Within the narrative, the first resurrection we witness is Geryon's photograph of a fly. Carson explains the document of Stesichoros' telling of the classic mythic story to stress that Geryon, the beast, was killed by Herakles in ancient times. This is a master narrative which Carson is recreating in postmodern terms as the queer mad messiah.

Thus, when Herakles "kills" Geryon by unceremoniously dumping him, Geryon's suffering is metaphorically documented in a photo. Geryon is emotionally crushed: "... weak as a fly Geryon crouched against the sink/ with his fist in his mouth/ and his wings trailing over the drainboard" (*Autobiography* 71). This melodramatic representation of heartbreak is made ironic in the way Geryon is associated with the fly while it is raining outside, setting the terms for the magical signification of Geryon's photo-based autobiography. As if to fortify the emotional death Geryon experiences, he takes a photo utilizing a fifteen-minute exposure of a fly in a pail of water; his finished photo shows the insect "Drowned but with a strange agitation of light around the wings." The prolonged exposure makes visible the dying throws of the fly in "agitation of light." Geryon's photo is analogous to the "shot" of a gun, which the fly, as the alter ego, magically takes for Geryon. In conjunction with a pun on the literal significance of the photo being "taken," Geryon's heart (life) has been taken.

The *punctum*, that which forgets, saves Geryon from death; the irony is that it "wipes the slate clean," so to speak, from which Geryon can rise, "resurrected" in his maturing messianic status. It is worth noting that this "wiping clean" may describe Geryon's unnamed geographical location. In fact, we may speculate that the punctum signifies the return of Canada's national trauma: namely its genocide of indigenous peoples. Canadians and Canadian policies daily "forget" about the history of false treaties, Residential Schools, the 60s scoop; every punctum of Geryon's narrative may indicate the forgetting that upholds Canada as a nation. In Geryon's story, Turtle Island may be one iteration of Britain's historical violences in Ireland, Scotland, its colonies, making Geryon's story stand as quintessentially Canadian.

According to Lacan, one's relationship to the symbolic, the systems by which we live including language and law, are vital agents of action that are essentially violent. So, when Lacan says that the "symbolic kills the thing" he wants to convey how psychically, the symbolic register (language and law, etc.) confronts the subject with his/her mortality. In that sense, Geryon's photo of the fly is a kind of killing and reveals something important about Geryon: Geryon's undead immortal status is maintained because the fly dies; the fly is a substitution for Geryon, made possible because of the narrator's ability to show the autist's literalness as metaphor through the technological device of photography. Because the autist would focus on the literal meaning of "the fly died," the autistic foreclosure of the NOF remains intact, while the metaphor speaks as poetry to the neurotypical reader. The poetic reading does not affect Geryon. The same can be said when we watch Braggs' hand in water in the video; we may see symbolic signification, but that does not change the literal water she feels. Every withdrawal into his photographic essay, every contraction of himself into his autistic self-representation, prolongs Geryon's life, or, in metaphorical terms, sustains his immortality and the unstable irony of his messianic status.

If Geryon the human can be seen as exhibiting autistic tendencies, and his secret is this mythic winged self that attracts the death sentence from which he is repeatedly rescued by his magic *punctum*, then the most compelling element of an autobiography is the photograph *sans punctum*. In McCallum's thorough analysis of the photographic revolution in Carson's text, she overlooks the anomaly of the double *puncti* in photograph #1748, subtitled, "It is a photograph he never took, no one here took it" (*Autobiography* 145). In this image, the narrator drops her authorial pants figuratively by using a comma splice while referencing a poem by Emily Dickinson, "1748: The Reticent Volcano Keeps"; Photograph #1748 is the most paradoxical moment in the autobiography and not just because the photo is considered a poem, but because the poem is not a photo that was ever taken.

A similar non-photo happens when Geryon flies over the eye of the volcano, far from the author's "here," "and he smiles for the camera" (145). In the Volcano "photo," there are two devices that are recording, the volcano's eye and Geryon's tape recorder, neither of which creates a photograph. As a self-document of Geryon, the photographic moment of the volcano exists only figuratively, and is encountered by the inside of Geryon only. What is literal of Geryon, what reflects the real as the impossible eternal, is operative in the following fact: the author who documents all outside things is noticeably "blind" to the "there" of the real document from "here" and is framed as missing and equal to the impossible idea of resurrection. The volcano's eye, the primordial undead real of it, apotropaicaly protects Geryon from being consumed by the volcanic flames—a sort of symbolic representation of the *Real* encountering the *Real*. It is as if Carson, the operator of the narrator's photography, has chosen to represent her own autistic nerve as that which returns again and again to exploit the magic of the literal. The mad messiah is the poet who saves the world through art.

It is not until Geryon flies over the volcano that we recognize his messianic status. When we read, "[h]e has not flown in years" (145), we are taken aback: there was no moment when we had seen him fly before now. Ironically, this moment in which we realize these wings actually function, retroactively interjects the *real* into the symbolic. In opposite terms, the symbolic disappears into the *real* when we read: "The Only Secret People Keep." The secret that this testimony keeps, because the author cannot represent it in language, is the recorded sound of the *real* entering the symbolic order: Geryon's flying. Apart from Geryon's survival, the only material document of this *real* flight is the audio tape that is something literally impossible to represent in print, bringing us to a moment of not "hearing things" as the audio of an autist "listening to himself." Moreover, the sound recording of an immortal winged being over a volcano is an intellectual feat that is equivalent to literary silences, pushing the NOF away as the poetic tension gestures to the silence of beyond. Thus, Photograph #1748 covers over the rupture made by Geryon's *real* immortality, after which, his messianic powers can be shared with Herakles and Ancash where they stand with "immortality on their faces" (146). For the reason this sharing supposes a kind of cure of autism through socialization, and because this text is a self-reflexive autobiography, this socialization happens on Geryon's terms as a transcendence enabled by the mad messiah that he is.

Monique Tschofen suggests that the end of *Autobiography* reflects a sort of transcendent moment, which "lets us reach beyond 'outside' things to connect with immortality itself" (40). While we can read Carson's fire as an idealistic retreat from the modernity of the camera to the primordial order, accepting Tschofen's interpretation would involve a misreading of Geryon's particular relationship to the technology of the camera, which points to Carson's role in this autobiography, and most importantly, Geryon's homosexuality. The volcanic fire, found in the baker's oven, the fire which is mankind's literal source of life and symbolic form of life, is the technology that describes the photographic process: an image is burned into the film with light of Geryon and his friends. They stand as an image of the trinity in the Christian faith:

the father, son, and holy ghost; the two thieves and Jesus. I argue that this baker's fire is the first photographic holophrasis of the physical truth of his messianism, pushing ironically at the Christian doctrine's condemnation of sexual deviance: homosexuality and bestiality. In that respect, the last photograph of three queer subjects, one of whom is a "beast," with "immortality on their faces" (146), deconstructs the Christian resurrection: echoing Geryon's photo of the fly in the throes of dying, this image is the substitute of that which the symbolic kills leaving Geryon free to exist in eternity with his friends. With the "night of the world" at their back, with the dark struggle of their soul behind them, the symbolic "New Beginning" of Geryon, the beast he was, has been transformed into the anointed messiah of the Catholic trinity.

The autobiography has enabled Geryon to be converted to the Oedipal camp, pointing to a prejudice that we unconsciously live with as modern secular neurotypicals. Moreover, whereas I have speculated that Carson sustains a partiality for the Canadian version of the Protestant narrative in "Book of Isaiah," I propose a Catholic tendency in *Autobiography*, which may indicate the Francophone political struggle against the Protestant ruling class, and beyond them, the white Anglo majority. In this scene before the oven, there are several reasons to see a Catholic twist. For one, the Catholic church is homophobic, making the presence of a gay trinity ironic as well as moving, if we see in this representation a recognition of abuse perpetrated by priests of the faith. For another, the trinity is before the bread baking oven, where "bread" in the Church is the eucharist, or holy flesh of Jesus, a principle not found in Protestantism. Is it possible that the prevalence of Catholic architectural culture in Montreal influenced Carson's representation of this figure? In Montreal, Catholic structures surround her, such as the hospitals L'Hôtel Dieu, the Convent in Mount Royal, St. Joseph's Oratory and the Notre-Dame Basilica in downtown. Or is it "scarcely possible" to see that Carson's messiah points to the return of a trauma associated with the Catholic Church that is particular to the province of Québec?

For the Québécois, what has been at issue since the conquest of New France by the British ruling class has been their subordination to what Coleman identifies as the floating signifier of Canada's "white civility." It is important to acknowledge that much has changed in Canada's ethnic and racial demographic since the Battle of the Plains of Abraham, but the institution of the ruling class as predominantly WASP settler[14] still dominates in unconscious ways. We can see the effect of this in the quiet revolution of the 1960s which saw the Québécois' trying to achieve equality with Anglo Canada by liberating themselves from Catholicism: as the Québécois' embraced secularism, they emulated the ruling class. When realizing they would never be considered equals, they launched a separatist campaign which culminated in the referendum in 1995 that shook Anglo Canada to the core. Separation was an existential threat to Anglo Canada's sense of nationhood, generally, and to the ruling class, in particular. The threat was compounded by Québec's interest in seeking an alliance with the United States. It may not have been that serious a threat, since the United States may not have accepted Québec into its national borders, but for the Anglo Canadian population, and the ruling class, it was a crisis.

But what does this Franco/Anglo conflict have to do with the mad messiah? Here I would like to take the speculation in a certain direction. Carson was writing *Autobiography* during the time of the 1995 referendum on the heels of the language laws in Québécois urban centers. It was also at this time that, in her interview by di Michele (1996), she mentioned Pushkin's poetry, and terms such as "worship" and "devotion." This discourse, layered with Carson's identification with Oscar Wilde in the figure of Geryon, shows how Geryon's Catholicism in the novel can be seen to push against Canada's white Anglo Protestant heteronormative hegemony. If Isaiah's Protestantism strengthens the ruling class, Geryon's Catholicism signals a struggle within the ruling class. In fact, I speculate that we can read Geryon's sectarian identification as a symptom of a trauma that never happened: specifically, Britain losing to the French in the Battle of the Plains of Abraham. That is, every day that Anglo Canada resists the outcome of the quiet revolution in

14 The majority of Canada's first ruling class was made up of British Anglican and Protestant subjects; they established "white civility." The WASP political founders of the nation remain the unconscious definition of Canadian identity, even though a large minority of Canadians identify as Catholic. Moreover, though many citizens self-identify as secular, because secularism is a veil for Protestant ideals, these Canadians promote ideals established by the ruling class.

Québec, it is calling into question what it won on the plains and asks: was it worth it? Geryon's story intimates this ambivalence.

While I make a case for seeing Carson-the-poet as the agent of Oedipalization that makes it possible for Geryon, the messianic poet, to live out his autistic life only partially caught by the symbolic order, I am still mindful of the Steinian allusions Carson works with and particularly Stein's autobiography using her lover as a veil. Is *Autobiography* Carson's autobiography? Perhaps Carson is on the autistic spectrum; perhaps she grew up with synesthesia and as a child had a difficult time reading the symbolic elements of the world around her; perhaps she identifies with Geryon the red beast because she has always felt to be in a skin that she had to hide from others; perhaps Carson learned the symbolic with difficulty which is played out with such wonderful quirkiness in her postmodern way. And perhaps not. It is not my place to say. And then again, is it a problem that she may be writing as someone who is not on the spectrum?

While Mad Studies has made possible problematizing the representations of people on the spectrum by people who are not, there are limits to the critique. I still hold that it is a dangerous move to tell a writer what they are authorized to write or not; for one, authority is already a loaded term that implies a hierarchy over knowledge. In that hierarchy, who decides? Added to that issue is the fact that as readers, the last thing we know is the author's biography and Carson is reticent to disclose much about her personal life. Moreover, sometimes the author does not know themselves. That said, if it is true that Carson Oedipalized herself through poetry of the autistic story, then we are reading work by a neurotypicalized autist writing a neurodivergent project.

Ideologically, Carson's *Autobiography* is geared to a North American audience and since Canada "dares not speak its name," it is obvious this novel is set in Canada, and not only for the Catholic/Franco politics noted earlier. When Geryon speaks of all the grass as "red," is Carson indicating a kind of homage to the maple leaf, the flag, the nation? That seems a stretch. Hard evidence for seeing Geryon's early life set in Canada is when he responds in the negative to the query, "You from the States?" He is not from the United States; since he travels to South American regions (Buenes Ares and Peru), he is not from there either. This naming of where he is going emphasizes how nameless his origin is.

Meanwhile, Herakles' comes from a place called Hades where a volcano periodically erupts, and which is a 7 or 4 hour drive away (arbitrary?) from where Geryon lives. It's unclear what city is referenced by Hades. Since Montreal is an Island with a mountain at its center, and there are bars where drugs are sold, we might suppose that Montreal is Hades, about a 5-hour train ride from rural Ontario. On the other hand, New York City is about a five to seven hour drive from Montreal and maybe it could have been considered a cauldron of cultural and drug activity. Speculation goes only so far, here.

Since Herakles' mother was a child in Mexico, we suppose Herakles's ethnicity is Mexican. The absence of any ethnicity in Geryon's home life suggests a kind of generic "white by default" making Geryon a member of Canada's white Anglo-Saxon settler community, one with the ruling class if only by race, and complicated by his pro-Catholic stance (the trilogy). His resistance to the dominant culture can be seen in how he defers again and again to the characters of ethnic minorities, such as Herakles, as well as Ancash. This difference could be a sign of weakness, or of absolute arrogance; he is a messiah, after all, with a privilege that he holds by birthright. Notice that birthright is a feature of nationalism, race and a messianic calling. While Carson maintains white settler color-blindness, she gives authority to a usually underprivileged subject, the autistic gay man, and thus throws a postmodern wrench at the heteronormative neurotypical narratives. The mad messianism of Geryon's gentle thought "we are amazing beings," indirectly creates equality. Of course, it's a quiet observation, equal in some measure to Canada's "Other" quiet revolution.

Conclusion

Carson's *Autobiography of Red* is a story of a mad messiah in terms that are somewhat different from "Book of Isaiah." Whereas in the latter, Carson relied on traditional biblical material, and the so-called Judeo-Christian tradition to enable a revision of the messianic narrative, the former secularizes ancient Greek myth turning it into a messianic story. Using this material, Carson's postmodern project aims to liberate the disenfranchised by dismantling fallacies around autism and homosexuality. I can see the latter fallacy being particularly poignant in the face of heteronormative Catholic policies. What it is saying about documented issues of the Catholic Church's refusal to address abuse in its ranks remains an open question. So, the messianic poet is liberating people from these soul crushing master narratives. But in what way? For one, Carson appears to be elevating Catholicism as a Canadian feature over the white Anglo-Saxon Protestant settler ruling class, but she is doing so in secular Québec riddled with language laws and separatist politics. This contemporary political climate highlights how much the Catholic faith is a symptom of the Anglo fear of losing ground in the conflict, a fear which is reinforced by the spectre of Québec's separation. But even if Geryon wears a Catholic robe, he is living in a place that "dares not speak its name" as the exemplar of white settler. As the figure of "white civility," he fails to destroy the master narrative of white rule; the most he does is show its weakness while conserving its hold on power. In contrast, Carson's treatment of psychosis is radical: through the "literary" device of photography, Geryon's autism is not totally subsumed by the neurotypical sensibility. The neurotypical "cure' is qualified and incomplete.

It should not be overlooked how much can be relayed about the unconscious in a given text: the unconscious of the author signaling the author's social context and era. As proposed, we are to see Geryon, the mad messiah, functioning in the postmodern text as a kind of beacon of opportunity; it takes on these Catholic features as if to liberate the Francophone community of white Protestant rule; but in the end, he accomplishes a conservation of Anglo power. In that move, we retroactively recognize that Geryon's Catholicism signals the Anglophone anxiety that Québec's separation will rewrite white Anglo victory in the Battle of the Plains of Abraham as a devastating and shameful failure. This is to say the sectarian features in Carson's messiah are markers of the ruling elite's inadequacy. Perhaps Québecers are aware of this feature of the Anglo elite; perhaps this feature is the root of Canada's widely recognized low self-esteem. Whatever may be said, it is clear that Carson's Geryon gives us some perspective on the Canadian unconscious.

Seeing Carson take on some autobiographical elements in Geryon's mad messiah narrative brings into focus one thing. We are not in a position to judge Carson's right to tell the story of an autistic subject.

She may very well be an autist and through maturation, learned how to fake Oedipalization. That could account for her particularly apt representation of neurodivergence in childhood, and her quirky post-modern deconstruction of the heteronormative neurotypical master narratives. Then again, we are speculating here.

CHAPTER 4

Messianic Failures

What does the end of postmodernism look like? For that matter, when did it end? I am going to suggest that the sequel to *Autobiography of Red*, *Red Doc>*, exemplifies that end. In fact, it is an example of what the last of the fruits of postmodernism looks like when it has gone to seed. The bloom of strategies has turned in on itself, folding into darkness; there is a hint of mold about to take hold. In postmodern fashion, *Red Doc>* undermines the idea that a sequel picks up where the last text ended, that the protagonist drives the plot, and that the narrator is an invisible aid to the story. For example, there is no sense that we're following Geryon in the next stage of his life; there are too many characters to figure out who the focus is, and for that matter, what the story is; the characters represent an array of mental health conditions from post-traumatic stress disorder (PTSD), to bipolar, to depression, anxiety, etc., articulated through the controlling obfuscating strategies of the narrator. The chaos that is *Red Doc>* even begs the question: what does this text have to do with the mad messiah I am going to argue is in this text? The messiah is hard to see, but in terms of a post-postmodern sleight of hand, it is there, hiding in plain sight.

In the pages ahead, I am going to highlight that in self-conscious terms, Carson undermines the postmodern master narrative of the mad messiah, itself, by showing that there are many candidates, all of whom are flawed. In turn, and in perhaps entirely unconscious ways, Carson maintains the function of the mad messiah in the text not through a character, but through the narrator. It is in considering the unconscious influence of her nationality on her text that I am also going to put pressure on seeing to what extent Carson's experience as a Canadian living in the United States has influenced *Red Doc>*'s construction.

Disabling the Sequel

The first postmodern move we see in *Red Doc>* is in how conflicted a sequel to *Autobiography of Red* it is. The latter is a *bildungsroman* about Geryon that claims to be an autobiography but in one critical respect is not: the story of his tortured relationship with the outside world, his first love who was Herakles who dumped him, and his reconciliation with Herakles in his early adulthood, are events told, not in the first person, but in a limited third person voice representing Geryon. *Red Doc>* similarly is told in the third person narrative position but abandons the focus on Geryon, now named G., who is a middle-aged owner of a herd of musk ox (or goats). G.'s central role in the narrative has been displaced by his connection with other characters: Ida who faked "bipolar disorder" to get out of charges for some undisclosed crime and Sad But Great, formerly Herakles, who is being treated for PTSD as a result of his time at war. 4NO also suffers from psychic war wounds. The story is relatively simple, if you can wade through the textual interference brought on by missing punctuation, sentence fragments, a chorus named Wife of Brain, and wandering characters. G. and Sad take a road trip to a glacier, from there they go to a mechanic's to get their car fixed, enter a psychiatric clinic named Ice-clinic run by CMO, a man who is a self-absorbed "devourer of other people's labyrinths." In the figure of CMO, it is worth noting a possible allusion to the Scottish Canadian psychiatrist Dr. Donald Ewen Cameron who, in the guise of curing mental health disorders in the 1950s and 1960s, ran experiments in developing mind control and torture techniques for the CIA at McGill University. At the clinic, Sad meets up with 4NO, a war veteran like Sad, who is being treated for complicated issues of anxiety. After a riot in the clinic happens, "they escape [the] same night" and on their road trip are being chased by slow moving lava. Eventually, they make it to the hospital where G.'s mother lays dying. The novel ends with his mother's death.

Critical responses to *Red Doc>* have been mixed. Some readers are totally enamored by the chaos Carson creates; others claim that Carson has gone off the rails with this one. Many critics have highlighted certain features of the novel that undermine generic expectations in extreme postmodern fashion. For example, Sam Anderson notes that "More difficult than *Autobiography of Red*, *Red Doc>*'s style is fragmentary, its pace herkey-jerkey, its rhythms of information trickier to pick up". The trouble with the causal logic of events of the novel leads Daisy Fried in her *New York Time's* Review to argue that the narrative "is not always to be moving forward, despite the velocity of individual pieces". Noted here is that pacing seems off; there are events and scenes that follow one another, but how they come together to inspire this forward motion, remains unclear. Yet attention to the structural experiments with syntax and narrative, which these critics have highlighted are the distinguishing characteristics of *Red Doc>*, interferes in clear access to a whole array of characters the majority of whom suffer a mental disability making each one a potential messiah. What needs to be acknowledged is that where Isaiah and Geryon were clearly protagonists in their texts, there is no central character in *Red Doc>*. Moreover, several characters have a mental issue, diagnosed or not, which means determining the actual messiah becomes a process of deduction.

Red Doc> is not a sequel to *Autobiography* because it is not strictly about G.; it is not about G. since, as Carson shows us in a scene mid-way through the novel, G.'s status as messiah is over. Sad, G and Ida "stare at one another all three of them wanting to grasp this moment where they are crowded like frozen travelers around a stove. Wanting a tiny burnished world and for a moment they glimpse it. Sad turns away" (91). G.'s power, what I had defined in *Autobiography* as messianic in his ability to share eternity with Herakles and Ancash, seems weakened by his inability to bring Ida and Sad to the fire of eternal life. And what they might see in that "moment" is not even defined. Where in *Autobiography*, we encounter the messianic moment as the transcendence of the fire of the baker's oven, in *Red Doc>* we find a muted (burnished) flame of messianism surrounded by "frozen travelers." If G. was the messiah in the former, G is not in the latter. Is it because he is no longer "mad"? Or perhaps it has to do with his spent youth. Early in the narrative, G. is looking at his mature self: "he glances at the mirror. Sharp stab his face no longer young no more beauty impact" (37). He no longer has a photographic narrative, but he still relies on image to center himself.

Other images come to his attention: namely, the Russian poet Daniil Kharms who pleaded insanity in order not to be sent to war, and was instead sent to prison where he died of starvation, "far removed from his own body." This leads G. to conclude: "No Jesus to cleanse it or koan to throw it off a bridge no Zeus to blast it to Tartaros" (38). G.'s messianic power has gone the way of his youth. Interestingly enough, while this would seem to cancel the postmodern messianic project altogether, other characters become eligible for the status simply for being mad.

The Real Messiah

Sad and 4NO are in the clinic being treated for war-related traumas: Ida is disqualified from messianic responsibility because she is not an "authentic" bipolar. I draw attention here to an unconscious misogyny in this text. All the main characters are men and Ida, the only woman, plays a supporting role to their narratives. The men are probably survivors of the Afghan war, which happens to have been fought by both the Americans and the Canadians from 2001 as a result of Bin Laden's attack on New York on September 11 of that year. The Canadian army was in offensive mode from 2006 to 2011. After that, they became trainers of the Afghan military before withdrawing in 2014. The Americans did not leave until the Trump administration tried to withdraw in 2021. PTSD was experienced by soldiers in both armies, though the Canadian soldiers' rate of PTSD was much higher than in the U.S. military. Since Carson, a Canadian, lives in the United States, and is exposed to the foreign policies of both nations, she would likely have enjoyed being ambiguous about which war, Canadian or American, each character fought in.

Sad suffers PTSD because, while at war, he witnessed a bomb killing local civilians. That trauma explains his living with a repressed memory that is so extreme it interferes unexpectedly in his present. Trying to cope with this psychotic break or a temporary lapse of sanity, he confesses to his difficulties:

> He said I can't sleep I can't remember what to think about when I'm sleeping I said why think just sleep. He said I found her bloody eyeglasses in the grass after nothing else was left not even. Not even what I said. Not even the stupid fuck white plastic shopping nothing her family could. (94)

We read the irregular and fragmented syntax, horrifying images, the hyper-reality of the images and the way phrasing cuts off this seeing, as signs of his trouble with keeping the past settled in the past, thus pointing to his madness. Sad's debilitating condition reaches its apotheosis at the clinic. Before the staged reading of 4NO's play *Prometheus Rebound*, Ida arrives with a white plastic bag that triggers Sad: "Sad … at this moment is staring at Ida and seeing the most grievous day of his life re-materialize before him" (105). The plastic bag brings up the memory of that horror he wants to forget and can't forget: Sad's past erupts in the present world of the clinic initiating chaos among the patients that comes to be known as the "riot" which causes the death of an elderly patient. Far from saving people from harm, as a messiah would, Sad's time-trouble seems to make him lethal.

4NO's time-trouble is also a condition caused by his time at war but is opposite to Sad's focus on the past: 4NO is focused on the future. Originally identified as F, 4NO suffered a crisis when he witnessed the mutilated dying of a boy named "Lucky" (48–50). "And from that moment F cannot stop seeing five beats ahead of time all the time for the rest of his life. Every minute is foreclosed. His present tense abolished" (50). Note the term "foreclosed": it references Lacan's symptom of the psychotic's refusal to accept the NOF in the Oedipal event. This is to say that since time is a signifier of order, just as the NOF is, then foreclosing time indicates psychosis. Notice also that the present tense is "abolished": it is not only not visible to 4NO, it has been destroyed. So as opposed to being a straightforward postmodern schizophrenic, caught by the "now," 4NO has a compromised relation to "now': "[the world's] entire future jumps into his eyes. Rooms always startle him. Doorways …" (96). The very gift Jameson claims is postmodernity, the schizophrenic's "now," eludes 4NO. Even so, he is messianic material, in respect to the postmodern mad messiah project.

4NO had foreseen that there would be an issue with the plastic bag when trying to stage *Prometheus Rebound*, but could not tell when it would happen so could not act in time to save people from harm. Prometheus, the figure who took fire from Olympus to give to humankind, is the first savior of mankind. 4NO, short for foreknowledge, is another name for Prometheus which explains 4NO's messianic aspirations. Prometheus' messianism involves planting "blind hope in their hearts" because "they were breaking" (109). Notice that the modern Prometheus is saving people not by giving fire, but by giving hope; people are no longer simply striving to survive; they are now in sophisticated conditions of heartbreak. What has broken their hearts is, as yet, unclear. But this condition explains the "rebound" mode of his story: a false opportunity is the way 4NO defines Prometheus's chances. Would this mean that 4NO's condition is troubled by the false opportunity of foresight to fix things? In point of fact, 4NO's condition ironically undermines his ability to save mankind.

Not only is 4NO not a Prometheus, he is also not Isaiah. A reference to Isaiah returns in Carson's *Red Doc>* through CMO's musings that 4NO is like Isaiah because of his ability to see the future. CMO asks, "Do prophets vary in their amplitude of vision? Maybe Isaiah had an oscillating variable of forty years or a century" (128). In comparison to Isaiah, though, 4NO's vision is not long enough. Yet in CMO's mind, 4NO is "better than Isaiah" because he "plays his cards close to his chest" (130). CMO is the kind of character you do not trust: he is motivated by his own interests and is extremely calculating, reinforcing my speculation that this figure is modeled on Dr. Cameron. In CMO's mind, 4NO is not as emotional as Isaiah, which is the outcome of the regimented world of army life. This suggests 4NO does not have the empathy to save humanity. In this sense, 4NO misses his messianic calling on two counts: being neither Isaiah nor Prometheus.

The Narrator Is Mad

I have essentially made a case for seeing no messiah in *Red Doc>* but I will now argue that there is a messiah: what the messiah's objective is, is not clear, which may be further to the plot trouble noted by its readers. The clue to the messiah is in Carson's critique of the master narrative of the postmodern schizophrenic's idea of time. That is, we can hear her propose that mental health conditions are not about an "eternal now" but about disordered time. The past and the future are represented by Sad and 4NO, respectively: the former lives in a past that troubles his access to the present, while the latter lives in a future that interferes in being in the present. In respect to the formal concerns of this fiction, these characters' compromised relationship to time obscures so much of the plot development. Fried claims that events happen without being "particularly inevitable" (Fried 4) and the next plot twist arises and disappears as randomly. She concludes that: "*Red Doc>* might fail as a novel—did it want to succeed as a novel?—but it succeeds as linguistic confrontation" (4). Is this the point of *Red Doc>*, to exploit experimental moves such as fractured syntax, non-sequiturs, ironic self-conscious asides, and disappeared quotation marks, to name a few formalistic details, simply as a postmodern requirement? I argue that these strategies are a way to represent the schizophrenic mind, a mind that is caught in what I would say is Carson's particular interpretation of a schizophrenic time, one that at first seems chaotic, but on review is extremely organized.

The narrator is in control of the trouble with time. It connects the complementary times of past and future of Sad and 4NO with a variety of "nows," one being the Wife of Brain which functions in the novel as a kind of chorus. There is also an ongoing dialogue, or many dialogues, that G. has with his mother ("Mildred taught me everything I know she taught me how to entertain" 30). Whether these dialogue "nows" are in the novel's now time or a now of a time before the novel's "now" time is unclear; their ungrounded place in the narrative adds to what I am defining as the novel's general chaos. Because these multiple times are all happening, sometimes at cross purposes, we are very aware of narrative control in *Red Doc>*. This literary coherence echoes Rae's observation about another of Carson's projects, namely "Glass Essay": "her seemingly fragmented poetry retains an element of rhetorical coherence and force... the paratactic shifts between topics, tenses, speakers, and narrative levels in 'The Glass Essay' produce what D'Agata calls a 'parallel present tense'" (183). In many ways, that "parallel present tense" describes how events, dialogues, descriptions, the Wife of Brain chorus, are collected as "all time" at once, or an eternity that Carson has recreated for the postmodern schizophrenic sensibility in *Red Doc>*. The fact that "Glass Essay" is considered an autobiographical project may suggest that *Red Doc>* is also autobiographical, a reason for putting emphasis on the role of the narrator in the novel. That is, through the narrator, we can hear Carson proposing that eternity is not no time nor an everlasting "now": it is actually all time all at once.

The narrator disrupts plot expectations and literary conventions in a way that one would suppose represents the psychotic's trouble with signs when in crisis. The use of the fragment is ubiquitous, as is the resistance to quotation marks. For example, the reader's first encounter with the enigmatic figure of Hermes, a silver suited phantom, is riddled with the fragment and a conversation that melts in the text:

> A human like form. Dressed in what could be a silver tuxedo. Shimmers faintly and pauses. Not glancing to either side. An intentness to it. See that says G. See what says Sad. Creek. Rush. Guns. The faint form seeps toward another fault in the ice and is gone. (44)

Fragments butt up against dialogue formally undifferentiated. In fact, here and elsewhere, speech spills out, overwhelming the reader, bringing to mind Lacan's definition of the psychotic as someone who is "spoken by the unconscious." In other words, the narrator is "spoken by the unconscious" and therefore mad. Going one step further, I am going to show that the narrator is not only mad; the narrator is the messiah of the novel. Just as Geryon was the poet messiah in *Autobiography*, the narrator of *Red Doc>* is the poet messiah.

So what does the narrator-as-mad-messiah accomplish? It is the narrator, not a protagonist, that brings about the story of fractured subjectivities that cannot be healed suggesting the mad messiah of the novel functions as a witness. The discontinuity of time experienced by the characters is not resolved by the riot, after which everyone "escapes" the clinic. The message here is that the clinic is causing the damage, or the clinic cannot heal them. They do not need healing or do they? The fact is, they all exemplify conditions from an ablest perspective on health: they are in an institution that is treating them with "illnesses." In fact, since no one is saved from their "illness," the narrator's role as messiah is problematized. On the one hand, it is a problem that the narrator would need to heal people from mental health conditions which may in fact be simply how their brains are now wired. And on the other hand, it signifies how the narrator is a failed messiah because it is not mad: the narrator's madness is pure conceit. Or, you could say, this conceit explains how the novel fails.

The constructed quality of the narrator's psychosis reflects a Mad Studies argument. The metaphorical use of schizophrenia for the postmodern project relies on stereotypes of madness by the neurotypical author. So, is Carson a neurotypical author critiquing her postmodern project by relying on a stereotype of madness? Or does her project critique the neurotypical theorists/postmodernists idea of the schizophrenic as a savior figure from a neurodivergent perspective? It is hard to say, but I speculate that the whole host of mad characters who are not "healed" by the clinic reflects attitudes by survivors and consumers of the Canadian psychiatric communities from the early 1970s and on. Is it possible that Carson was cognizant of the criticism against the psychiatric community in Canada, a criticism that was circulating at McGill because of Dr. Cameron's CIA project?

It is worth speculating that Carson is alluding to Cameron in the CMO, considering the prevalence of the cultural currency of his infamy over the last 40 years. For example, in the 1980s, the *Fifth Estate* aired an episode interviewing two former patients whose lives, one could see, had been permanently derailed by the abusive treatment they endured in Cameron's care. In 1988, Ann Collins *The Sleeping Room: The Story of the CIA Brainwashing Experiments in Canada* came out about Cameron's treatments and a decade later, a tv series adaptation directed by Ann Wheeler, *The Sleep Room*, aired on television. More recently, in Naomi Klein's *The Shock Doctrine* (2007), Dr. Cameron's name again appears: Klein proposes that his treatment of patients was primarily focused on developing torture techniques. Whether or not we can see in the CMO character of the novel a critique of psychiatric care in Canada, we can definitely see Carson self-consciously representing the postmodern schizophrenic as a narrator faking madness. In that sense, Jameson's schizophrenic is a false savior, the messianic project has gone to seed, the narrator's bloom of youth has given way to deep wrinkles.

Mortality

Perhaps it is the headiness of the characters affected by ECTs, drugs, or other psychotropic remedies, that explains how the novel lumbers along in fits and starts with barely a sense of a story arch. So, if this is a novel, the first question we would ask is "what is the crisis?" If we knew the crisis, then perhaps we would understand what the mad messiah needed to accomplish. And it is hard to say, except when we arrive with G. and his companions at the hospital where his mother is, we start to feel we are on a bit more secure ground. The crisis of the novel, in fact, that which should have been the focus but was not because Sad and 4NO and Ida and CMO obscured it, is G.'s mother's dying. But G.'s mother is Carson's mother, because as with the "Glass Essay," *Red Doc>* is an autobiographical project which is why the poet appears. Fried notes the shift: "Suddenly there's a poet behind the mask of G, a poet whose mother is a quandary to avoid and submit to" (4). Carson's mother had recently died. Canadian poet and critic Margaret Christakos claims the entire book is about Carson grieving her mother's death: "Anne Carson is a master of untelling... Grief is the master, and a master of disguises and aliases begetting misrecognitions and retributive reversals as tragic subjects flail for a clarity that detests itself." What Christakos names grief I name madness and maybe Carson is equating grief with madness—a madness that has the effect of spreading chaos across the narrative.

Both Christakos and Fried recognize the presence of the poet in the text. This is also when we can see that Carson is the narrator who is performing madness. The scenes with mother are gentle. There is no semantic interference, or not much. We hear her speak, we see her movements. The distortions have subsided, and she is clear and in focus. She reminds Sad of the pearls he wore to the prom which shows us that her memory is intact. She is still concerned with how she looks, indicated by her asking G. to pluck her facial hairs: "There are hundreds thousands. He hates waiting for her to wince. It's alright Ma you can hardly see them he says. Her eyes fall. *Okay never mind*" (154). Notice the use of italics for speech, which is a direct allusion to *Autobiography of Red*. We can "hear" when G.'s mother is talking, so uncharacteristic of the kind of soup of dialogue we see in the first part of *Red Doc>*. And then his mother dies and G. is at the house packing away her belongings.

It has been raining: "Rain continuous since the funeral a wrecking rattling bewildering Lethe-knuckling mob of rain. A rain with no instructions" (160). The signature fragments employed with the paratactic strategy give us a sensory experience of the deluge, while the allusion to Lethe, the river in Hades that when drunk makes the dead forget their past, offers us a figurative reflection on G.'s fear that in death, his mother will not remember him anymore. The more interesting reflection is the following line: "rain with no instructions." Neither rain nor tears hold instruction about how to grieve. Rain is of the natural order but in coming into contact with the human order is made unnatural, sometimes, when its "surfaces" … "sound like they're sliding up" as if defying gravity. Can defying gravity be equal to defying mortality? But the messiah's responsibility is to defy death. That is the master narrative that Carson undermines. She puts into the narrator's hands a madness whose messianic project is not to free people for everlasting life, but to witness the end of life, and the broken hearts left behind. The poet messiah is Carson's grieving wish to save life from death, a wish we might see deeply buried in 4NO's play *Prometheus Rebound*, as the wish to give hope to the broken hearted. When a mother dies, one's heart breaks.

In an interview, Carson admits that, in contrast to the fulfilling experience she had writing *Autobiography*, *Red Doc>* was "a mess, obstacle course, uphill grapple in the dark, almost totally disoriented experiment every minute of the thousand or so years it took to work out" (Anderson 22). Carson's hyperbole highlights a troubled process that has left its mark on a project that seems intent on exposing the postmodern strategy of psychosis to be a pretense of literary liberation or justice. Can we see that where *Autobiography* succeeded, *Red Doc>* is its sequel by failing? Perhaps that is Carson's final postmodern move. The messianic power of the mad narrator is to blow up the schizophrenic "now" and show that there is no such thing as salvation, that G. was never in a position to be Daniil Kharms's savior (83), that eternity is disorienting and grief is the only life after death which the hands of the narrator, the poet messiah, cannot save us from.

Christakos reads *Red Doc>* as overwhelmed with the death of the mother at the end. This is supported by what we recognize as these periodic moments of G.'s dialogue with his mother interspersed throughout the novel. On further consideration, though, we can say "death" is everywhere in the *Red Doc>*, from the event that traumatized Sad to the experience 4NO had, to what happened to G.'s cow "Io," to Hermes's appearances foreshadowing death. These expressions of death may be said to exemplify Carson's conscious and unconscious grief. In that sense, the death of G.'s mother may very well stand for the end of

Carson's postmodernism: the mad messiah does not have the power to keep mother from dying; the mad messiah of postmodernism stumbles when it faces death, creating chaos; the mad messiah cannot save G. from his grief, not even by telling a fabulous story in which time overwhelms us with what we imagine is the texture of eternity. No, the narrator's literary madness fails leading to the narrator's final thought, a self-conscious confession: "not every day can be a masterpiece" (163).

Where Is Here?

With each geographical place in this novel, from the fields where the ox roam, to the glacier, the mechanic's, the Ice-clinic, the black sea, the volcano and mother in a boat-sized bed, a generic and even imaginary "there" appears, since none of these places locates us in a recognizable city, much less nation. The fields with sassafras where G. lives with his Ox, could be anywhere in rural North America. The internal locations of the clinic and the mechanic's shop and the hospital, seem "generic" urban. Looking closer at each locale, defining where we are appears less complicated. The fact that 4NO needs to work for CMO to "pay off his bill at the clinic" (96) puts us on U.S. soil, since Canada's health system is, for the most part, publicly funded. So how does Sad get away with not paying anything? Is he there on some U.S. veteran's program, or do we see a reference to Sad's and G.'s youth growing up in Canada where many health services are free? Some, such as dental and eye care, are not. It is impossible to locate this story definitively.

The locations of the events seem to be near a glacier-cum-volcano. Is this landscape imaginary or real? Geographically, the majority of volcanos are located in the "ring of fire" region, essentially around the Pacific Ocean: the west coast of United States or Canada is on one part of that circle. But then on the Atlantic side, there is Iceland which has the largest number of glacier/volcanos, the largest one in the world being in Vatnajökull National Park. That said, there are many active volcanos on the west coast of North America, including Mount St. Helens and Rainier in the United States and Mount Meagre and Baker in Canada. In this novel, where are we? Is this the "nation that cannot speak its name," that is, the self-effacing Canada otherwise articulated by Stephen Cain's paraphrasing of Henighan as "a new ahistorical internationalism," (*Reading the Postmodern* 117)? I would suggest that the "here" could very well be an international version of Canada, the everywhere that is here. The Canadian geography I am confident of are the scenes at the hospital where G.'s mother lays dying and the home where G.'s mother lived: these scenes point to Carson's autobiographical reflection on her mother's death. Maybe we can say the rain is Canadian, and I say this ironically. It would suit Carson to see rain as having no geographical boundaries. In that respect, it is worth considering that Carson wants to obscure the location to account for both Canadian and American locations, perhaps emblematic of her being a Canadian having lived in the United States for decades.

In this sequel, we are deep in the non-partisan kind of culture that we associate with secularism. But the fact is, as some scholars have argued, secularism is an ideology modeled on Protestantism and suits the white settler sensibility. Prometheus is a modern revision of the Christian Jesus stripped of its religious details. Alongside this secularization of ancient Greek mythology is the de-sectarianizing, or secularizing, of the biblical prophet Isaiah. In other words, in these cases, we can see the mad messiah is witness to the shattering of the grand narratives of Greek mythology. Both Prometheus and Isaiah are disguising the politics of the dominant class, an idea amplified in the novel by the fact that the Catholic trinity of eternity that defined the end of *Autobiography* as a Francophone idea, disappears in *Red Doc>* with Geryon's loss of trinity power. What is striking is how Carson's secularizing of Greek Myth reiterates that unconscious conservation of the white Anglo-Saxon (Protestant) settler that we see in both *Autobiography* and "Isaiah." Carson's work does not shatter "white civility," but cements it. But how do we know this secularism is Canadian and not just generically North American?

It is true that we have no geographical details in the text to indicate if we are in Canada or the United States or simply North America. The characters' citizenships being unspecified do not help us, either. Furthermore, no one's ethnicity is defined in this text, apart from Malekh, whose name and "accent" give him away as a "foreigner," someone not from "here." The foreigner, in fact, gives us some hint of a North American immigrant demographic. But whether this social geography is indicative of the multiculturalism we find in Canadian society, or the melting pot of U.S. society, is unclear. Besides Malekh, everyone else seems to speak with the same accent, including Sad who, though Mexican or perhaps part Mexican by heritage, seems integrated in society as a second-generation Latino. Thus, the majority of the characters are ethnically the same. The generic features of the players in this novel means they are mirrors of the culture that dominates in North America, that culture being settler of mixed ethnic and racial origins who have "converted' to the expectations of the white ruling class.

At this point the most we can conclude is that the postmodern messiah in *Red Doc>* is Anglo-white settler, or Anglo-white passing, that is, second-generation immigrant. We can speculate that this novel's Canadian as opposed to simply North American location is evident in small features of the narrator. The fact that the narrator as poet tries to save all the characters and essentially fails would support the kind of postmodern irony that Hutcheon claims is typical of the Canadian postmodern. In the fusion of Isaiah and Prometheus in 4NO, we find a parody of the messianic, which returns us to Hutcheon's definition of Canadian postmodernism. Moreover, the narrator's disabling of both time and syntax is what Avant-Garde poet Christian Bök would say is the ultimate expression of the Canadian postmodern. With all this said, we need to acknowledge that the strategies identified by these Canadian scholars about Canadian literature may be shared with our neighbor to the south, again making the issue of nationalism unclear.

But one feature about *Red Doc>* that makes it Canadian is Carson's resistance to naming where it is happening, and who is acting, signifying a self-conscious self-effacing. In that sense, representing the messiah as a narrator is the ultimate self-effacing move. Canadian identity is reinforced by the fact that the narrator/ poet messiah is "stateless": in other words, it hails from a "nation that dares not speak its name." That might be considered a significant unconscious move on Carson's part, reflecting on her sense of statelessness with the loss of her maternal connection to the land. But this statelessness could be indicative of Canada's sense of shame. In his *Negative Review* series, Shane Neilson discusses our national shame, outlining how Canada's culture has always been determined by its inferiority complex compared to the United States and Britain. It has shame in producing work that cannot compare to the U.S. cultural industry, shame in being the inadequate offspring of

European (British and French) cultures, and in more contemporary terms, shame in being white settler. Perhaps this is why Canada's literary culture prefers "internationalism": this "everywhere" erases its inadequacies against its relatives, but more importantly absolves it of its national crimes against indigenous peoples. So, the mad messiah in Carson's work is indicative of a Canadian shame.

In another sense, Carson's project is a very Canadian one by defining itself against American culture. Specifically, it deconstructs what I would claim is the American version of the postmodern master narrative: the Jamesonian schizophrenic. If Jameson's cultural schizophrenic is all about "now," Carson's messiah is a narrator who generates "all time all at once." *If* this is schizophrenia. And that is what the text pushes us to question, in our mad effort to understand: maybe we are being afflicted by a neurotypical vision of madness. What I am saying is that Carson may be seen to want to expose Jameson's schizophrenic liberation as a fallacy: in the process of playing the madness card, she undermines the postmodern project for liberation from ... well, Jameson called it capital; Carson, in the cases we have seen, associates it with mortality. Whatever the project, postmodernism's death can be said to have started with Mad Studies criticism against the exploitation of madness in culture which I would suggest has manifested in the narrator's contortions of time in *Red Doc>*. In critiquing postmodernism from a Mad Studies perspective, *Red Doc>* is radical.

Carson's particular deconstruction of the messiah in *Red Doc>* supports Mad Studies scholars' complaint with Jameson's metaphorizing the schizophrenic condition. I would argue this critique is in dialogue with survivor and consumer movements in Canada's history of psychiatric care. Moreover, the failure of Carson's messiah may be considered a symptom of Canada's shame in being unsophisticated, provincial and white Anglo settler. To what extent Carson is aware of what she's doing and to what extent she is unconscious, is beside the point: the fact is, in *Red Doc>*, she has drafted another spectacular specimen of a messiah that is quintessentially Canadian.

Conclusion

di Michele's aversion to Carson's interest in "devotion," "praise," and "worship," or in other terms, religious ideas, points to a general resistance in secularism to religious discourse in the public domain. It is a resistance that Carson's work pushes against while she tries to dismantle the grand narratives of madness and heteronormativity in her postmodern fashion. What the pages before revealed is that Carson's religious interpretation of the Jamesonian schizophrenic gives us what I am defining as the mad messiah. This figure has shown us the traumas emanating from the Canadian secular unconscious, showing us which master narratives fall apart and which won't.

The Mad Messiah

The primary criterion for my selection of Carson's texts was the mad messiah. The secondary criterion was chronology; I chose texts that corresponded to three different periods in her writing life which happened to show a kind of story arch of postmodern culture. In the early period of her writing, or the early stages of postmodernism, "The Book of Isaiah" was an opportunity to explore her treatment of the religious, which was too often overlooked by secular minded writers such as di Michele. *Autobiography of Red*, an award-winning text, exemplified the middle period of her oeuvre: we can read it as an apotheosis of her engagement with the postmodern. Carson translates or reinvents the postmodern subject as a figure on the spectrum; their conversion to a neurotypical sensibility is enabled through the technology of photography. *Autobiography* is also a text that made explicit the issues raised by Mad Studies about the appropriation of the neurodivergent protagonist by the neurotypical writer. We have a story to read thanks to the neurotypical narrator without which, Geryon, the red winged beast, the autistic homosexual as the mad messiah, would not exist. *Red Doc>*, as the failed sequel, reflects what I propose is signifying less the last period of her career, than the end of postmodernism's schizophrenic subject. Madness, as a monolithic conceit, has splintered into a number of conditions by a variety of characters who are each competing for our attention, making the narrative aimless. What does the mad messiah accomplish in this text? Well, it goes without saying that it does not save Geryon's mother from death. Then again, who is to say that the text itself does not immortalize her, vanity aside, or vanity included, and in that sense, is messianic.

Carson's work is postmodern, so her task is to undermine the master narrative: there is Isaiah, the prophet who becomes a messiah, reflecting the monotheistic tradition from the Christian perspective, and what he accomplishes is nothing more than a self-absorbed kind of transformation. As I have speculated, Carson's messianic prophet, believing he can save the world, reflected aspects of Daniel Paul Schreber and Louis Riel. Whether Carson did this consciously or not us up for debate. What is striking about this representation of Carson's postmodern schizophrenic, the mad messiah, is that it is very human and less exploitive than Jameson's theory invites us to think the figure might be in culture. That is, by seeing Isaiah as a schizophrenic, the master narrative of divine revelation collapses into human fallibility; at the same time, anyone who has had the distinction of receiving divine messages, is not to be denigrated. Carson's telling exposes the stigma against madness while it reinvents madness as empowering. Thus, in one respect, Mad Studies would find "Book of Isaiah" a valuable revision of the biblical text; in another sense, however, the exceptionality of this figure stands out as false, and not at all in touch with the reality of people who are diagnosed with schizophrenia. If we accept divine revelation as a positive reflection on madness, the text offers a positive outlook on the exceptionality of madness. But underlying this narrative is the neurotypical argument that divine revelation is the only justifiable madness.

Autobiography of Red rewrites Jameson's postmodern schizophrenic character as on the psychotic spectrum, and specifically, the autistic subject. I find Carson's choice to engage with the autistic subject interesting, partly because autism was only just becoming a prevalent diagnosis in the 1980s, and also because neurotypicals see autism as a condition that begs for a "cure," or some kind of rehabilitation. High functioning autists manage to do well in mimicking neurotypical expectations; that is, they have "converted," if uncomfortably. Thus, Geryon passes for neurotypical while he hides his bestial wings, coming out only at the end when taking a photo that was never taken, over the mouth of the volcano. Ironically, the way that Geryon comes out as a beast contrasts with the way he comes out as gay in the narrative; the unselfconscious way in which homosexuality is portrayed in *Autobiography* might suggests that Carson relies on ancient Greece's long and public tradition of queer life.

Carson secularizes Herakles myth through the tool of photography; the shoot, the shooting, the killing is converted in the unstable irony of the narrative as the catching, saving, immortalizing of Geryon in photographs. Geryon, the autistic subject who lives outside of human time, the mad messiah, is saved through the lens of the camera, and at the end, offers his friends immortality through the fire of the baker's oven as the punctum of the photographic shot. That is, the messiah is the poet whose poetic death is life (i.e., resurrection), a conceit rooted in Christian teachings. In this inventive way, Carson's mad messiah undermines the grand narrative of Greek heroism by secularizing it and deconstructs the master narratives set by neurotypical heteronormativity by reinventing a new way to see autistic queer subjectivity. While that may be how the novel offers us a radical reading of madness, it also asks us whether we as readers can judge who has the right to represent madness.

Red Doc>'s characters are ethnically generic, but with respect to mental health issues, represent a spectrum of conditions. On the one hand, we can see something positive about giving voice to this variety of conditions which have generally been silenced under the vague rubric "mental health issues;" on the other hand, there is an ableism voiced here, in seeing all these characters at the clinic in need of "healing." That requirement for healing calls attention to the one orchestrating the whole project: the narrator which, as I have pointed out, is a failed messiah. Not only is the narrator not mad, it also does not fulfill the greatest expectation of a messianic figure: it does not free us from mortality. Granted, Isaiah couldn't accomplish that either and Geryon accomplished only a moment of immortal transcendence. But if the messiah brings equality, in the secular sense, then the narrator as mad messiah in *Red Doc>* may be said to accomplish that by showing death as the only equalizer of all living things. The failed messiah's revelation does not work as a moment of convergence for the different characters and their plots: it merely works as a little island of recognition in the chaos of this book. And since Geryon's mom, as we recall, is a white woman, we have simply slid back into Carson's conservation of white Anglo-Saxon (Protestant) settler dominion. In that sense, the mad messiah of *Red Doc>* may accomplish its role as witness to death, but it fails to break down the grand myths of Canadian settler rule.

The Canadian Unconscious?

What can Carson's mad messiah show us about the Canadian unconscious and what can it tell us about the nation's trauma? Remember, the messiah is a return in secularism of a trauma of injustice. The mad subject is the one that has been defined as demanding equality and in some ways, that has been addressed by her mad messiah. It has done so by deconstructing grand narratives about madness, both madness in social terms, and madness in postmodern culture. When it comes to looking at what Carson's mad messiah can do with Canadian myths, we see little effect except to reveal several traumas that are layered from the least to the most unconscious: that is, ableism, the Franco/Anglo conflict in Quebec, and the crimes against indigenous people, respectively.

In all of the texts we've reviewed, what stands out is how secularism is one of the grand narratives that underpins the rule of the elite class. In *Autobiography*, Catholicism is a symptom: it is used to indicate a white Anglo anxiety about the rise of Québec nationalism that, in embracing secularism, sought to become equals with the Anglo majority. Apart from Malekh in *Red Doc>*, no character's ethnicity stands out as distinct, making everyone "white" or "white passing," a condition that can be applied to second-generation immigrants or indigenous people who have learned the code of "white civility," a code enabled by secularism which, in the process of aiming for equality, strips Prometheus of divine power. The Jewishness of Isaiah is erased; we don't need to see Isaiah represented with brown hair and blue eyes to recognize that he is as whitewashed as Jesus in the west. Even when Carson tries to get in some strange visions of a "deer" in "Isaiah," an American adoption of an Levantine gazelle, we are caught by the false inclusivity of the Judeo-Christian paradigm, the Jew taken over by secularism, itself a formula modeled on Protestant ideals that shore up the white Anglo-Saxon rule. So, while the mad messiah may carry out some interesting critique of madness, when it comes to undermining the grand narrative of Canada's secular promises and Protestant authority, it does little damage. If anything, the mad messiah reinforces Anglo rule.

It is noteworthy that we can see a Canadian, not American, culture in this project because the characters are located nowhere in particular. Since every story seems to be set in an "anywhere," an International anywhere at that, we have evidence for seeing Canada's self-effacing setting as "a nation that dares not speak its name." Does this predominant "erasure" of geography, social, political and physical, express a Canadian trauma? We might consider Coleman's reflection on how the heroism of the white male subject belies the historical record of the mistreatment of indigenous peoples and minorities. This is to say that not only is there a racial preference for the white settler, that preference is also for the masculine subject, suggesting an unconscious reinforcement of patriarchy in Geryon's work. As well, situating the story nowhere means that we can read a silence covering over the "white man's" guilt for being on stolen land. The crime does not have to be addressed if no one says anything about it. This silence speaks volumes of Canada's transgressions.

It is tempting to suppose the United States and Canada are similar in being governed by a white Anglo-Saxon Protestant elite, while embracing "foreign" cultures such as French, Irish, Italian, Greek, Portuguese, and more recently, Asian, South-American, Middle Eastern, African, peoples, etc., as a false equality. What is false about this ethnic equality, which distinguishes Canada from the United States, is the authority Canada's white Anglo elite exerts over the Francophone community, an authority rooted in the historical struggle founding Canada. Québec's push for independence, and its language laws in the 1980s and 1990s, are historical issues that call attention to an almost two centuries long fight by the Franco communities of Québec against the ruling class's domination, both economically and politically. In speculative terms, I have proposed seeing that Carson's Catholicism in *Autobiography* is symptomatic of the return of a repressed historical moment in Canada's history, namely the battle of French and English colonizers. From the perspective of the British winner, the fear of having lost all along rises with the talk of Québec separation.

While it is heartwarming to see Geryon problematize heteronormative neurotypical perspectives in *Autobiography*, it is still disturbing to see how the mad messiah upholds an Anglo settler culture. The same may be said for the mad messiahs in *Red Doc>*: there is a problematizing of the postmodern schizophrenic's false "now," but Malekh is there to uphold the fact the dominant culture is white, or white passing. In all cases, the erasure of the geography of these narratives highlights a Canadian shame: even as a writer who has "escaped" the misogynist small-minded community of English poetry in Canada, thinking specifically of Solway and his ilk, Carson continues to white-wash locations and characters in her work. Moreover, as is evident in her ambiguous representation of the Afghanistan war, much of her Canadian culture has been fused with U.S. culture which we could say is emblematic of a Canadian standard for marketing Canadian content. Canada's self-erasure is a ploy to get U.S. audiences to see themselves in what we sell. Or, we might propose it is symptomatic of the trauma of Canada's cultural identity. From the beginning of its formation, Canada has had to resist threats by U.S. foreign policy (manifest destiny) and cultural industry (Hollywood). In one sense, we can say Canada's generic qualities signal the behavior of a chameleon: if it hides its colors, it will not be recognized as a threat; if it looks like the enemy, it will not be threatened by enemy invasions, either. But there has been evidence for seeing a Canadian unconscious running through the messiahs. The most poignant and perhaps considered by some as the most far-fetched speculation is seeing in Isaiah an unconscious representation of Louis Riel, not as a story of Métis power, but of a historical moment that is full of settler guilt, so deeply buried it is almost invisible.

Trauma persists on many levels in her mad messiahs. Trauma is that sectarian rift that begins with the Battle of the Plains of Abraham in 1759, one in which Québec concedes to British rule, and from that day, becomes a minority in the Canadian nation. The quiet revolution can be seen as the return of the trauma of that battle; by embracing the secularism of white Anglo rule, in abandoning their faith, French Québec can be said to have tried to erase their difference from the English and thus show themselves as intellectual and cultural equals. So when Carson has Geryon engage in the cultural power of the eucharist, she means to deconstruct secularism's promise of false equality, but in the end she restores secularism through Geryon's last words; when Isaiah's secularization stands for the first religious narrative about Jesus, he is ultimately promoting a white colonizer's narrative; where the narrator of *Red Doc>* tries to resolve the madness brought on by death, it is ultimately conceding to the white Anglo Protestant/Anglican elite as the status quo. No matter one's faith, Canadians agree to accept secularism, its covert Christianity, as the norm. Canada's founding elitism maintains its power over minorities, never willing to give ground—at least not in Carson's work. You might say, the Canadian trauma in Carson's poetry is symptomatic of how the white settler class struggles to maintain its power by perpetually promising equality to the "other," and continually reneging on the promise.

A master narrative that remains invisible by the mad messiah is settler shame and this shame points to a trauma that has no voice. Where Québec's sectarian trauma could at least be vocalized by religious discourse and separatist politics, settler guilt is buried in the silence expressed in the generic whiteness of characters living in the "nation that dares not speak its name." By not locating the narratives in Canada, Carson's texts are silent on the original trauma of this nation: its crimes in displacing and murdering indigenous peoples. That silence perpetuates the dominant Canadian myth that we bought the land fair and square and indigenous people are being treated well. The fact her work sustains this myth is not a criticism of her work, by any means: it is an observation highlighting how unconscious traumas are shadows in the text, legible for their absence, heard for their silence, and how projects like the mad messiah, those that mean to change the order of things, are limited.

Maybe *Red Doc>* exemplifies how Carson gives up on postmodernism as a method because she recognized that, as a poet, she could not break down the most deeply rooted myths of Canadian identity and its politics. In that sense, we may see Carson conceding to the limits of postmodernism as early in her career as Isaiah whose hermaphroditism is temporary and fruitless: nothing changes, everything stays the same. The mad messiahs fail, and not because they are mad, but because grand narratives cannot fail.

Bibliography

Anidjar, Gil. “Secularism”, *Critical Inquiry* Vol. 33, No. 1 (Autumn 2006) pp. 52–77.

Benjamin, Walter. “On the Concept of History.” Trans. Harry Zohn. *Walter Benjamin: Selected Writings Volume 4, 1938–1940*. pp. 389–98.

Blankholm, Joseph. *The Secular Paradox: On the Religiosity of the Not Religious*. New York: New York University Press, 2022.

Betts, Gregory. “*Non Compos Mentis*: A Meta-Historical Survey of the Historiographic Narratives of Louis Riel’s ‘Insanity’,” *International Journal of Canadian Studies/ Revue internationale d’études canadiennes* (38) 15–40.

Carson, Anne. *Autobiography of Red*. New York: Vintage Boos, 1998.

Ibid. “Anthropology of Water” in *Plainwater*. New York: Vintage Books, 1995.

Ibid. “Book of Isaiah” in *Glass, Irony and God*. New York: New Directions Books 2005.

Ibid. *Red Doc>*. McClelland and Stewart, 2013.

Coleman, Daniel. *White Civility: The Literary Project of English Canada*. Toronto: University of Toronto Press, 2008.

Di Michele, Mary. “Anne Carson *The Matrix* Interview.” *Matrix* 49 (1996): 11–17.

Freud, Sigmund. *Moses and Monotheism*. Trans. Katherine Jones. New York: Vintage, 1967.

Igartua, Joe. *The Other Quiet Revolution: National Identities in English Canada, 1945–71*.Vancouver: UBC Press, 2006.

Hutcheon, Linda. *The Canadian Postmodern: A Style of Contemporary Canadian Fiction*. London: Oxford University Press, 2012.

Jameson, Frederic. *Postmodernism: Or the Cultural Logic Of Late Capitalism*. Durham: Duke University Press, 1991.

Lacan, Jacques. *Seminar III: On Psychosis*. Trans. Russell Grigg. New York: W. W. Norton and Company, 1997.

Ibid. *Seminar XI: The Four Fundamental Concepts of Psychoanalysis*. Trans. Alan Sheridan. New York: W. W. Norton and Company, 1998.

McCallum, E. L. "Toward a Photography of Love: The Tain in the Photograph of Anne Carson's Autobiography of Red" *Postmodern Culture*. 17.3 (2007): 1–66. Web.

Rae, Ian. *From Cohen to Carson: A Poet's Novel in Canada*. Kingston: McGill Queens University Press, 2008.

Schreber, Daniel Paul. *Memoirs of My Nervous Illness*. Trans, Ida Macalpine. New York: New York Review Books, 2000.

Stacey, Robert David, ED. *Reading the Postmodern: Canadian Literature and Criticism after Modernism*. Ottawa: University of Ottawa Press, 2010.

Žižek, Slavoj. *The Sublime Object of Ideology*. London & New York: Verso, 2008.

Index

Reimagining Canada

Editors: Gregory Betts (Brock University), Carl Everton James (York University) and Ian McKay (McMaster University)

Canada, in all its messy manifestations, is in transition, but where is it going? With foundational myths eroded, identities fragmented, allegiances contested, the idea of Canada in the hearts and minds of those who live there is under intense scrutiny and careful criticism. Canada's place in the wider world is just as uncertain. Against a backdrop of COVID, Indigenization, decolonization, inflation, immigration, and shifting global politics, what might Canada mean in five, ten- or fifty-years' time?

Reimagining Canada seeks to understand the forces at work, and to ask what comes next. Taking a broad and inclusive approach to the study of Canadian culture, history and society, the series interrogates Canada's past and present in order to suggest possibilities for the future. Relevant issues might include, but are not limited to: arts and culture; Indigenization; decolonization; digital spaces and media; the future of the Canadian constitution; globalization; healthcare and social services; immigration and multiculturalism; memory and memorialisation; and sovereignty.

The series is open to scholars and public intellectuals working in all areas of the humanities and social sciences, and aims to be interdisciplinary or even post-disciplinary in its approach. The editors are committed to equity, diversity and inclusion and welcome contributions from scholars of marginalized groups and communities that tend to be disproportionately underrepresented within public discourses in Canada. As such, they strongly encourage scholars from these groups and communities to contribute to the series. Contributors are free to self-identify as desired.

Books in the series are aimed at a more general audience than the traditional academic monograph. Readers might include undergraduate students, academics working in other fields, practitioners, policymakers, and the public. The series provides a platform for authors to reach a larger audience than usual, or to speak to new audiences; to deliver bold new arguments; to write unencumbered by the usual obligations for referencing; and to be exciting, provocative and even polemical.

Published Volumes

Mad Speculations: Anne Carson's Messiahs and the Canadian Unconscious
By Concetta Principe

www.peterlang.com

Zeitfracht Medien GmbH
Ferdinand-Jühlke-Straße 7
99095 Erfurt, Deutschland
produktsicherheit@kolibri360.de

Druck:
CPI Druckdienstleistungen GmbH
im Auftrag der
Zeitfracht Medien GmbH
Ein Unternehmen der Zeitfracht - Gruppe
Ferdinand-Jühlke-Str. 7
99095 Erfurt